W9-DEA-400

Expert Systems and Artificial Intelligence
in Internal Auditing

*Dedicated to my children
who let me better understand
the process of
knowledge acquisition
on a daily basis.*

Dan

EXPERT SYSTEMS AND ARTIFICIAL INTELLIGENCE IN INTERNAL AUDITING

by
Daniel E. O'Leary, Ph.D., C.P.A.
Paul R. Watkins, Ph.D., C.M.A.

Advanced Information Systems Program
School of Accounting
University of Southern California

WARNER MEMORIAL LIBRARY
EASTERN COLLEGE
ST. DAVIDS, PA. 19087

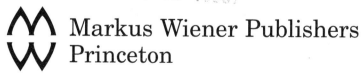

Markus Wiener Publishers
Princeton

12 -18 -97

HF 5667.12 .0433 1995
O'Leary, Daniel Edmund.
Expert systems and
artificial intelligence in

© Copyright 1995 by Daniel E. O'Leary and Paul R. Watkins.
All rights reserved. No part of this book may be reproduced or
transmitted in any form or by any means, electronic or mechanical,
including photocopying, recording, or by any information storage and
retrieval system, without permission of the copyright holder.

For information write to:
  Markus Wiener Publishers
  114 Jefferson Road, Princeton, NJ 08540

Library of Congress Cataloging-in-Publication Data

O'Leary, Daniel Edmund.
    Expert systems and artificial intelligence in internal auditing/
Daniel E. O'Leary and Paul R. Watkins.
    (Rutgers series in accounting research)
    Includes bibliographical references
    ISBN 1-55876-086-5
    1. Auditing—Data processing. 2. Auditing, Internal—Data processing.
3. Expert Systems (Computer science) 4. Artificial intelligence.
I. Watkins, Paul R.   II. Title.   III. Series.
HF5667.12.0433   1994   94-16674
657'.458'0285633—dc20   CIP

Printed in the United States of America on acid-free paper.

Contents

Chapter 1

INTRODUCTION

This book investigates the use of artificial intelligence (AI) and expert systems (ES) in internal auditing. In particular, the book addresses the roles of internal auditors in the development and use of AI/ES; the diffusion of AI/ES among internal auditors; and the impact of AI/ES on the status of internal auditors. This investigation was sponsored in part, by the Instituts of Internal Auditors (ITA).

Overview of Artificial Intelligence and Expert Systems

Artificial Intelligence can be defined as having a fundamental goal to enable computers to exhibit human-like intelligence or solve problems that humans solve. Given this general goal, AI includes a broad array of concepts/techniques which include robotics, computer vision, theorem proving, natural language processing and expert systems. Much of the current research and development efforts for applying AI to business applications appear to be in the area of expert systems (ES) and to a lesser extent, natural language processing (NL).

Expert systems are prominent as applied artificial intelligence systems since the focus of ES is on developing computer programs which perform in a manner similar to a human expert in a particular domain of expertise or application. A traditional definition of ES is a computer system that has an expert's or specialist's knowledge about a particular topic represented (programmed) in a specialized database (knowledge base), which has a mechanism, called an inference engine, for controlling the reasoning process through that knowledge base. The knowledge base typically is composed of facts and rules for solving problems. The inference mechanism is typically designed to make inferences during a consultation of the user with it. These inferences are made based on the input data of the user and the information stored in the knowledge base.

1

Many ES do not have solely the specialized knowledge of an expert embedded within the computer program but are systems which may also embed general knowledge in order to achieve more "intelligent" decision aids or decision support systems (knowledge-based systems). This "non-expert" knowledge may be that knowledge found in procedures and policy manuals, books, opinions of staff and other sources. For purposes of this study, *ES are any knowledge-based systems, expert or non-expert, in which the knowledge and inference components are separated and which are developed using AI/ES methodology.*

Expert Systems have been the focus of a great deal of recent attention by government, business, academia and the media. As a result, expectations are high, and some confusion exists regarding the nature of applications suitable for ES and the scope of such applications for ES. Further, guidance often is needed regarding appropriate development and management strategies for dealing with ES technology in organizations. Internal auditors, in their unique role within organizations, are now or will become consumers and auditors of, managers and consultants for, and even developers of the technology.

Internal Auditors and ES

Internal auditors and their management need to be aware of the issues involved in dealing with ES and related AI technologies for their particular organizations. Each of the five roles of internal auditors relating to technology (auditors, consumers, developers, managers and consultants to management) is now briefly described with emphasis on the internal auditor's role relative to AI technology. These roles lead to a number of questions that form the basis of investigation in this study.

AUDITORS

In the internal audit function a variety of auditing activities are carried out. With respect to these audit activities and AI, the following non-exhaustive list of issues and areas of concern needs to be addressed:

1. Auditability of the expert system. One expanding role of internal auditors may be to assess the quality of ES technologies throughout the organization. As such some of the following topics need to be considered:

a. How do you audit a knowledge base?

2

b. How do you assess the reasoning mechanism (inference engine) of the ES?

c. How do you assess reliability of the ES? That is, does the ES produce consistent results when the same inquiry is put to it slightly differently? Does it produce consistent results if rules happen to fire in a different order because of accidental factors in the knowledge base such as the order in which rules are listed?

d. How do you validate the ES in terms of "correctness of judgment"?

e. Is there a strategic plan in place for evaluating the current state of knowledge in the knowledge base (that is, is there a plan for monitoring and updating, as necessary, the ES's knowledge)?

2. Plan for establishing design and development standards with respect to appropriate security and controls. The internal audit function should have a framework or set of guidelines for insuring that proper controls are implemented during the design and development of the ES.

a. Are appropriate controls in place during development of ES to allow you to place reliance on the ES's advice?

b. Has explicit recognition been given to the different implementation environments of ES technology such as "shells" vs. symbolic programming in LISP and the potential implications for developing appropriate controls? (For example, some ES may be separate workstations programmed in a symbolic language such as LISP and, as such, are one-user systems. Other ES may be extensions of current MIS or decision support system and may be written in a procedural language such as "C" or COBOL and, as such, are perhaps multi-user, distributed processing based systems.)

c. Is the system secure from potential intruders and unauthorized use?

CONSUMERS

As internal auditors begin to acquire and use the AI/ES technologies in the internal audit function, a number of issues can be identified that require attention. Some of these issues include:

1. Strategic planning for establishing application priorities.

2. Methodology for selecting suitable applications for which to apply AI technologies. For example, the following two topics may be of significant interest:

    a. Management's concern with white-collar crime. (Is ES technology suitable for decision support in detection and prevention of white-collar crime?)

    b. Risk management of the internal audit function. (Can ES technology be utilized in the assessment of risk and in the allocation of limited audit resources for auditing high risk areas?)

3. Plan for assessing the various ES products and tools available and acquiring the technology. Strategy for determining whether to develop from scratch or buy shells or other tools.

DEVELOPERS

In some cases, internal auditors may be directly involved in the development process. This involvement may be for development of ES/AI for internal auditing independent of other systems development groups in the firm or it may be in conjunction and cooperation with other systems groups. Several issues are described below:

1. Do we hire the AI talent to develop these systems, contract with AI vendors, use consultants and/or do we train our own staff in AI technology?

2. Do we have a method for estimating labor costs and development times for ES projects? (Typically measured in person-years!).

3. Do we have realistic expectations with respect to what is desirable versus what is feasible? Can cost/benefit analysis be appropriately used to assess this issue?

4. Is there a plan for assessing where we want to be with respect to ES development? That is, do we want users to develop low-level expert systems using shells (the microcomputer spreadsheet analogy) or do we wish to have the development process controlled by centralizing it or by use of other means?

MANAGERS

The internal auditor may be required to manage the AI technology within the internal audit function. The scope of management activity may range from ES project development (and thus project management) activities to managing the end user use of ES technology. Appropriate policies and procedures need to be established for the management of the AI/ES technologies within the internal audit function.

CONSULTANTS

The internal auditor is increasingly being cast in the role of an internal business consultant. As such, expertise in all the above areas may be required in order to properly guide non-audit management's attention. For example, AI and related information technologies are causing dramatic changes in the work environment such as the proliferation of end-user computing using micro-computer workstations. The internal auditor may be required to advise management on the "management of change." In addition, the internal auditor may be in a position of generating policies and procedures for the use of AI/ES.

A Theory of Roles

Accordingly this book investigates a theory of roles in the activities of the internal auditor in the development and use of AI/ES. It is found that five different roles are useful in capturing the set of issues and applications resulting from the use of AI and ES by internal auditors and their organizations.

In particular, internal auditors operate as: consumers of AI/ES; consultants to management regarding AI/ES; developers of AI/ES systems; managers of AI/ES systems; and auditors of AI/ES. Each of these roles plays an important role in organizational change using AI/ES. These issues are discussed in more detail in Chapter 5.

Diffusion of AI/ES among Internal Auditors

What factors influence the adoption of AI/ES by internal auditors? One approach used in this book is the "economics of diffusion." The model used in this research is one based on the economics of diffusion (e.g., Rosegger [1980]). In that model, a variety of factors are thought to be related to the adoption of technologies, including environment, organizational and the nature of the particular innovation. The analysis found that adoption was related to development support, firm-wide pressure to adopt the technology, a lack of budgetary pressures, the potential for manpower reduction, the certainty that the adoption will improve the audit process, the lack of potential for disruption of other departments and whether or not the use of the technology can be accomplished in an inexpensive manner. These issues are discussed in detail in Chapter 6.

Impact of AI/ES on Status

Another approach to the adoption of AI/ES is its impact on status. In particular, the driving force in the analysis of this research question is "to what extent are changes in status related to the adoption of AI/ES." The research on this issue is based on the theory of exchange in social situations. In particular, it was found that its changes in status are positively related to technology adoption, the ability of the technology to provide benefits, the number of EDP auditors, the pressure to adopt and the information flow about the technology. Status was not related to changes to the budget in correspondence to the technology. These issues are addressed further in Chapter 7.

Audit and Security of Expert Systems

Internal auditors often are viewed as responsible for the security and audit of AI/ES. Unfortunately, at this time there has been only limited research on those issues. However, this paper provides some initial research into auditing and securing expert systems. The approach used here is to identify the unique aspects of expert systems and design tests to facilitate the audit of expert systems. In addition, those unique aspects provide a basis for generating additional approaches for securing those systems. These issues are discussed in detail in Chapter 8.

Outline of this Book

This book proceeds as follows. Chapter 2 summarizes the methodological approaches used in the book. Chapter 3 provides a literature review of the use of AI/ES in auditing and previous surveys on auditing. Chapter 4 summarizes a series of interviews that the researchers had with developers of AI/ES applications. Chapter 5 analyzes the different roles that internal auditors have with the design and implementation of AI/ES systems. Chapter 6 provides an economic analysis of the diffusion of AI/ES among internal auditors. Chapter 7 investigates the relationship between technology adoption and status. Chapter 8 provides some guidelines for the security and audit of AI/ES systems. Chapter 9 provides an "Executive Summary" of the book.

Chapter 2

METHODOLOGY

The methodologies used in this study included, literature review, interview and surveys.

Literature Review

An extensive literature review was conducted to determine the use of AI/ES in internal auditing. Since the literature in internal auditing was somewhat limited, and since developments in other forms of auditing were viewed as closely related, a broad based survey of the auditing literature was generated. The literature review is summarized in Chapter 3.

Interviews

In order to facilitate the development of a questionnaire and the understanding of the use of AI/ES by internal auditors, a series of interviews were conducted by the researchers. A number of firms were identified by the Institute of Internal Auditors as either using, developing or investigating the possibility of the use of AI/ES in internal auditing. Interviews were conducted with the internal audit department head or the head EDP auditor.

The interviews were conducted using open-ended questions. Much of the open-ended discussion resulted in questions for the survey. For example, in the case of a few firms, the interviewees indicated that one of the primary reasons that AI/ES was being adopted was because of firm pressure to adopt the technology. The interviews and the interview process are discussed in more detail in Chapter 4.

Survey

A survey was used to gather data to test information about each of the three major issues: roles, diffusion of AI/ES and impact on status of AI/ES. Appendix A contains a copy of the survey and summary values of the variables.

RESPONDENTS

A survey instrument was developed and sent to 3,267 department heads of internal audit departments. These department heads were members of the IIA. The names and addresses were obtained from the IIA. The surveys were sent with a cover letter from the IIA director of research, indicating the importance of responding to the survey.

SURVEY INSTRUMENT

The survey had three different parts. First, information was gathered on the background of the subject (industry and size, such as number of internal auditors and EDP auditors). Second, information was gathered about the different roles of internal auditors in the context of AI/ES (consumer, consultant, development, management and audit of AI/ES). Third, information was gathered on the adoption and use of ES, and the impact of AI/ES on the status of internal auditors.

The survey employed both open-ended questions and categorical questions of, e.g., three options (e.g., None, Some and Extensive). Throughout, since the respondents were practitioners, the number of categories was limited to a maximum of four categories, in order to ensure return of the questionnaire by the respondents.

The survey was pretested for validity and completion time. The instrument was reviewed by another faculty member and the Director of Research for the IIA. Based on those reviews, minor changes were made in the overall format and questions. It was estimated that, excluding the open-ended questions, that the average completion time would be about 5 to 10 minutes.

USE OF INTERNAL AUDITORS AND CHOICE OF TIME FRAME

Internal auditors were chosen for two primary reasons. First, the opportunity arose to study internal auditing. The IIA issued a call for proposals for an investigation of "...the issues and applications of expert systems and artificial intelligence for internal auditors and

8

their organizations" (quoted from the cover letter to the survey, signed by R.B. Muirhead, Director of Research at the time of the survey). This allowed access to internal auditor department heads. Second, there has been limited research about internal auditors. This leaves a gap in knowledge about internal auditors. Thus, this research sought to mitigate that gap.

The study took place in 1988, a time frame also was chosen for a number of reasons. First, similar to the use of internal auditors, the call for proposals was issued and implemented at the request of the IIA. Second, the first applications to auditing and internal auditing appear to have occurred in 1983. By focusing on the state of adoption as of the end of 1988, there had been a five-year time horizon. Such a time frame is required for the usage of an innovation to diffuse (e.g., based on previous diffusion studies [Rosegger 1980]. Third, 1988 was the first year that revenue from knowledge-based systems tools exceeded $100 million dollars, while, venture capital investments "... plummeted to ... zero" (Burton [1991, p. 66]). It was at this time that "AI winter described the state of the artificial intelligence industry: cold, dark and dying" (Burton [1991, p. 66). Fourth, this was the year that many companies began shifting away from AI programming languages to ES shells, and when both mainframes and workstations, began a rapid increase in use (Burton [1991, p. 66]). Thus, there were beginning to be major changes in the industry.

The choice of 1988 might concern someone interested in trying to merchandise expert systems using these findings. Otherwise, from a research perspective, the date allows us to retrospectively ensure both sufficient understanding of the diffusion captured in our study, and the completeness of the action/event set (e.g., activities by IIA) affecting the diffusion.

RESPONSES

Since the quality of the responses was a function of familiarity with ES, the last question in the first part of the questionnaire asked the respondents if they were familiar with ES. If the respondents had "no familiarity," they were asked to stop.

Of the 3267 survey instruments, 918 were returned for a 28% response rate. No follow-up mailings were made because of the nature of the agreement with the IIA. Of the 918, there were 909 usable responses. Of those 909, 406 indicated familiarity with expert systems (12.4% of total).

RESULTS

The results of the survey are summarized in Chapters 5, 6 and 7.

Data Analysis

The survey resulted in two types of data to be analyzed. There were categoric responses to the questions and there were open-ended questions.

CATEGORIC DATA

The data generated by the survey was categoric. A log linear model (e.g., Dixon et al. [1988]) was used to analyze the categoric data. Further details are available in Chapters 6 and 7.

OPEN-ENDED QUESTIONS

The open ended questions resulted in responses that were classified by the authors. The process used was as follows. First, one of the researchers categorized the data. Second, the other researcher substantiated the categorizations. There were few differences between the two sets of categorizations.Furthur details are provided in Chapter 9.

References

Burton, C., "Experts Say AI Freeze is Beginning to Thaw," *Computerworld,* July 29, 1991, p. 66.

Dixon, W., Brown, M., Engelman, L., Frane, J., Hill, M., Jennrich, R., Toporek, J., *BMDP Statistical Software Manual,* University of California Press, Berkley, Ca. 1988.

Rosegger, G., *The Economics of Production and Innovation,* Pergamon Press, Oxford, 1980.

Chapter 3

LITERATURE REVIEW OF EXPERT SYSTEMS IN AUDITING*

The approach of this study was to first review the literature on the audit environment and then on the use of expert systems and decision support systems in auditing. Because of the broad nature of internal auditing, research and systems in all aspects of auditing were investigated. Of course, in a study of this type, there are likely a number of references and systems that have not been included because of the broad base of the location of information on these systems and the rapid proliferation of publications describing these systems.

Different authors (e.g., O'Leary [1986]) have noted that expert systems have a number of different purposes. They can be used to assist the decision maker, replace the decision maker or train the decision maker. To-date, the major advances have focused on assisting the decision maker, although this chapter also discusses systems aimed at replacing and training decision makers.

The Audit Environment

The audit environment is a unique and highly complex decision-making environment. This implies there are sources of error and inconsistency that are unique to the audit environment. Personal computers and other changes in technology have had and will continue to have an impact on the audit environment. In addition, the audit decision-making environment is process oriented and not results oriented.

---

* An earlier version of this chapter was published in the *Expert System Review,* Volume 2, Numbers 1 and 2.

COMPLEXITY

The audit environment is highly complex. In a discussion of that complexity, Hansen and Messier [1982] note that the audit problem of determining control weaknesses is a "nondeterministic polynomial" problem. This indicates that audit problems have a large number of solutions and that it is difficult to sort through those solutions, in order to chose the best one. Such problems often are solved best by using heuristic approaches to find "good," but not necessarily "optimal" solutions. In the case of audit problems, this generally means using rules of thumb of experienced auditors. Since such rules of thumb can be included in expert systems, such systems offer an alternative and feasible solution methodology to auditing situations.

SOURCES OF ERROR AND INCONSISTENCY

Holstrom [1984] identifies thirty-two different sources of error and inconsistency. Holstrom [1984, p. 1] states the following:

> Judgment errors occur when there is a departure from a generally accepted criterion. Judgment inconsistencies occur whenever there is a difference between judgments, given the same data set and objectives, regardless of whether a generally accepted criterion exists. An error in overall judgment occurs when the auditor issues an incorrect audit opinion. An inconsistency in overall audit judgments occurs when different auditors render significantly different audit opinions based upon an identical set of financial statements and an identical set of audit evidence. In the latter case, we could determine that an inconsistency has occurred, but we could not conclude which overall judgment is in error unless we know in fact whether the financial statements were materially misstated.

Research (e.g., Hogarth [1985]) has shown that computer programs, such as expert systems, can be used to improve the consistency of human responses and mitigate errors. For example, as noted by Dillard and Mutchler [1987b, p. 17] "Utilization of the ... (expert) ... system will lend consistency, thoroughness and verifiability to the audit opinion decision process."

PERSONAL COMPUTER ENVIRONMENT

One of the primary developments in computing is a shift toward a personal computer (PC) computing environment. Researchers (e.g.,

O'Leary [1986]) noted that the change to the PC environment can have a major impact on auditing. First, the PC allows the users to take computing power with them to various locations. As a result, expert systems can now be developed to support the auditor in the field. Second, since so much work is now done on PC's there is increased need to be able to audit in a PC environment. Expert systems can be used to bring auditing knowledge to the auditor for the audit of PC-based systems.

CHANGING TECHNOLOGY

Holstrom et al. [1987] identified "...numerous trends that are likely to have a major impact on audit evidence, the audit process and the role of auditing in the next 10 to 15 years." They summarized the changes in information technology in four different categories: Office Automation and Transaction Automation, Data Communications, Computer Hardware and Computer Software.

Their initial results indicate an increased use of expert systems in auditing in the future, as exemplified by some of the applications discussed latter in this paper. In addition, it is likely that expert systems will be used to mitigate some of the problems resulting from, e.g., the move toward a paperless society. For as the "Law of Requisite Variety" (e.g., Ashby [1965]) notes, it takes equivocality to remove equivocality. Accordingly, as there are changes in complexity in those four categories, the systems needed to process information from those systems also must be more complex.

As a consequence of these large-scale and rapid changes in technology there is a major impact on training auditors to deal with these new technologies. Since few auditors currently in the field have received formal education in these technologies, there is a substantial need for auditors to receive some kind of training or flow of information on these technologies.

PROCESS ORIENTED—NOT RESULTS ORIENTED

Many problems in auditing do not have feedback mechanisms that provide for the recognition of correct or incorrect responses (Kelly et al. [1987]). Accordingly, instead of being results oriented, auditing is process oriented. The quality of the work is not judged by results, but by the record of the process as summarized in the work papers.

Expert systems can be used to promulgate a particular audit process and record work done during that process. Thus, they can provide uniform documentation of the process and act to defuse knowledge to the auditors.

ORGANIZATIONS

There has been limited research on the organizational impact of expert systems. O'Leary and Turban [1987] examine some of the possibilities. However, there are some unique such concerns that can be critical to the audit environment. These include the following:

The auditor has a different relationship with the rest of the organization than other groups within the organization. Often the role as an auditor forces them to maintain an arms-length perspective.

Since auditors rarely directly impact the production of goods, they are regarded as an overhead function. As a result, management often can be restrictive in the allocation of resources to the audit function.

The organizational structure of an audit team is definitely hierarchical in nature. Typically, the team reports to some level of management and the team itself employs a number of levels of audit personnel.

In addition, many of the tasks of the audit team are accomplished relatively independently by the team members. The independent activities are then assembled into the audit report. As a result, audit tasks are often "loosely coupled."

Expert Systems and Decision Support Systems in Auditing

INTRODUCTION

The purpose of the remainder of this Chapter of the book is to examine the current state of expert systems and decision support systems in auditing. In so doing we will examine completed or prototype expert systems and decision support systems in both external and internal auditing, including special areas of focus such as EDP auditing and governmental auditing.

This Chapter focuses on those auditing-based systems that have appeared in the literature or have been presented at a conference or of which the authors are currently aware. There may be some systems that have been developed and are in use, but are not reported here. Generally, that would be because there has been little information on those systems in the literature.

This chapter does not provide a general overview of expert and decision support systems. Such treatments are available from a number of sources including Hayes-Roth et al. [1983] and Moeller [1987].

In addition, this chapter does not discuss or try to differentiate between expert systems and decision support systems. Both types of systems support audit decision making and, thus, both are included in this paper. The interested reader is referred to Turban and Watkins [1986] for such a discussion.

PREVIOUS LITERATURE REVIEWS

There have been a number of other literature reviews of accounting and audit-based expert systems and decision support systems in academic outlets, e.g., Amer et al. [1987], Bailey et al. [1987], Bedard et al. [1984], Borthick [1987], Chandler [1985], Dillard and Mutchler [1984], Messier and Hansen [1984] and O'Leary [1987]. There have also been a number of surveys of audit-based expert systems in professional outlets, e.g., Bailey et al. [1986], Borthick and West [1986], Elliot and Kielich [1985], Flesher and Martin [1987] and McKee [1986]. However, these surveys generally have ignored intrusion detection type systems, internal auditing and governmental auditing. In addition, there has been a structural change in the development of expert systems since those papers were written. The first reports of expert systems in auditing were almost entirely from academics. Now, it seems that many of the systems that are generating the most interest are systems developed for commercial purposes.

These commercial systems differ from systems developed by academics in a number of ways. First, they are not just developed to see if such a system can be developed. They generally are designed with the idea that they ultimately will be used. Second, commercial ventures usually entail the use of greater resources then can be mustered in most academic-based expert system developments. Third, in commercial efforts, the application is dominant. Methodology issues, design issues and other research issues are the primary focus of many academic systems.

PLAN OF THIS CHAPTER

This Chapter proceeds by reviewing, respectively, audit-based expert systems in EDP Auditing, External Auditing: Academic Systems, External Auditing: Commercial Systems, Governmental Auditing and Internal Auditing. Limitations of auditing-based expert systems are then discussed followed by a discussion of sources for publication and presentation of information relating to expert systems. The final section provides some summary remarks.

EDP Auditing

Expert systems developed for EDP auditing take two primary formats. One approach is to develop an expert system to assist the auditor in auditing the system. Another approach is to develop systems that audit use of the system, in order to determine if there has been intrusion into the system.

AUDITING GENERAL EDP SYSTEMS

One system that has been developed to assist in auditing general EDP systems, is EDP-XPERT, been described in three primary papers (Hansen and Messier [1986-a, 1986-b] Messier and Hansen [1992]), which, respectively, describe the system and the validation efforts that were given the system.

EDP-XPERT was one of the first auditing-based expert systems on which development efforts initiated. Early discussion of that system was given in Hansen and Messier [1982] and Messier and Hansen [1984]. EDP-XPERT was developed using the rule-based, expert system shell AL/X.

A sample rule from EDP-XPERT is as follows (Hansen and Messier [1986-b]):

If

1. Message Control Software is Complete and Sufficient, and

2. Recovery Measures are Adequate, and

3. Adequate Documentation is Generated to Form a Complete Audit Trail,

Then there is strong suggestive evidence that controls over data loss are adequate.

This system demonstrates that rule-based expert systems can be used to aid the auditing of internal controls in EDP systems. However, as noted in a related inquiry, Biggs et al. [1987] found that EDP auditors generally do not use "if ... then ..." rules of the above type. However, such rules may be constructed from knowledge acquired from those auditors.

SPECIFIC EDP-BASED APPLICATIONS

MIS Training Institute has developed a number of "expert systems" to assist internal auditors. At the time of this writing there were at least seven applications available, four of which are based on IBM systems. Those four systems focus on CICS (based on IBM's communications system), System/36 and "Expert Auditor System/38" (two IBM minicomputers) and IMS (IBM's database environment). While, three of the systems are more general and are concerned with data center reviews, disaster recovery and auditing microcomputers.

Each of the systems they have developed reflects at least three of the guidelines of a "good" expert system application (for example, O'Leary [1986]), thus providing empirical support for those theoretical observations. In particular, each system is based on a set of audit concerns about highly specific environments, each of the systems are the concern of a large number of auditors, each system operates in a PC environment and each of the applications are in areas that require a substantial amount of specific expertise.

These systems are smart questionnaire systems. Each of the systems apparently makes use of a sequence of interrelated questions.

INTRUSION DETECTION SYSTEMS

An important aspect of auditing EDP systems is ensuring their integrity. Expert systems have been designed to provide continuing, on-line "intrusion–detection" protection of EDP systems. Such systems stay resident in the computer system, monitoring the behavior of system users.

Denning [1987] has discussed such a system. That system is based on the hypothesis that exploitation of systems involves abnormal use of the system. Thus, by detecting abnormal use of the system, security violations can be detected. There are a number of examples of such violations, including the following (Denning [1987], Richard [1983]).

Attempted Break-in: Someone attempting to break-in to the system likely would generate a large number of illegal passwords.

Successful Break-in: If an illegitimate user successfully breaks into a system then they may have different location or connect time than the legitimate user on whose account they have accessed the system.

Penetration by a Legitimate User: A legitimate user interested in penetrating the security of the system might execute programs different from or in a different order than would be expected.

Leakage by a Legitimate User: A legitimate user that attempts to leak unauthorized data might employ a remote printer, not normally used, at a time of the day that also is unusual.

Virus: A virus may cause an increase in the storage used by executable files or an increase in the frequency of execution of files.

Typically, normal behavior is represented using profiles for each user or facility. Then behavior is compared to those profiles to determine if it is normal or abnormal. Abnormal behavior is then flagged.

A research area with substantial potential impact is making such systems more efficient and effective. This research requires the investigation of the efficiency of different intrusion detection strategies. Generally, this means determination of those variables that best signal intrusion and those means (for example, statistical) that best determine the levels of those variables that indicate intrusion. Further, it is unclear what the impact of context (a given firm) is on both variables and methods of investigation. In addition, it is unclear what the organizational impact is of such systems. For example, if intrusion-detection systems are used do human "detectors" continue to function or do users just say "oh, the system does that?"

Academic-based External/Internal Auditing Systems

Projects of concern to internal and external auditors have received the most extensive attention. In this area there have been a number of applications, including:

Adequacy of Allowance for Bad Debts—Chandler et al. [1983], Dungan [1983], Dungan and Chandler [1983, 1985], Braun [1986]

Audit Planning—Kelly [1984, 1987]

Going Concern Process—Biggs and Selfridge [1986], Selfridge [1988], Selfridge and Biggs [1988] and Dillard and Mutchler [1986, 1987]

Internal Controls—Meservy [1984], Gal [1985], Meservy et al. [1986], Bailey et al. [1985] and Grudnitski [1986]

Materiality—Steinbart [1984, 1986]

Risk Assessment—Mock and Vertinsky [1984, 1985], Dhar et al. [1987] and Peters et al. [1988]

ADEQUACY OF ALLOWANCE FOR BAD DEBTS

The first audit-based expert system was developed by Dungan [1983] (see also Dungan and Chandler [1983, 1985]) to analyze the problem of the adequacy of the Allowance for Bad Debts for large commercial clients, based on analyzing the accounts individually. The system, entitled AUDITOR, was developed using the rule-based expert system shell AL/X.

AUDITOR gives advice in the form of an estimate of the probability that a given account balance will prove to be uncollectable. That research study had as (Dungan [1983]) "... its objective the creation of an expert system model of certain judgment processes of auditors." AUDITOR employs rules acquired from expert auditors. Associated with each rule is a probability that the conclusion in the rules (the "then" part) would occur given the evidence in the rule is found to exist (the "if" part). The system then provides an estimate of the probability that the account is uncollectable, given the evidence it is provided.

A second prototype expert system, was built by Braun [1986]. In some respects it is an extension of AUDITOR (Chandler et al. [1983]). However, the emphasis of the Braun [1986] study was on the hospital industry. In addition, it also considers the combination of analytical and judgmental variables.

As noted by Dillard and Mutchler [1987], output from systems like the one described here could be used as input to other systems in order to take advantage of development efficiencies.

AUDIT PLANNING

Kelly [1984, 1987] developed a prototype model ICE (Internal Control Evaluation) to aid in the audit planning process. ICE featured a knowledge hierarchy of three different levels. The first level included knowledge about the industry, economy, management and the audit history. The second level focused on the client environment, the organization, planning manuals, and accounting procedures. The third level focused on internal control functions in the purchasing process.

ICE was developed using LISP. Unlike most expert systems, ICE made use of both frames and rules.

GOING CONCERN PROCESS

The going concern problem is one of the most difficult facing auditors. As noted by the AICPA [1988] "in order to render a going concern judgment, the auditor must 1) recognize that a problem exists, 2) understand the cause of the problem, 3) evaluate management's plans to address the problem and 4) render a judgment on the basis of whether the problems are sufficiently serious and whether management plans are judged to succeed.

There have been at least two academic efforts to address the going concern problem. Both the work of Biggs and Selfridge and the work of Dillard and Mutchler can be traced in a series of papers describing the systems' changes over time.

Probably one of the most sophisticated accounting and auditing expert systems is GCX (Going Concern Expert) discussed in a sequence of papers by Biggs and Selfridge [1986], Selfridge [1988] and Selfridge and Biggs [1988a, 1988b, 1990]. GCX was programmed in MacScheme, a dialect of Lisp, that runs on an Apple Macintosh II. GCX was tested on five years of data from a real world company, about which the auditors who were questioned had substantial knowledge.

The research questions addressed in the development of GCX included (Selfridge and Biggs [1988a, p. 2]):

What are the categories of expert knowledge and how are they represented?

What are the reasoning strategies of the expert auditors and how are they represented?

How is the knowledge and reasoning strategy organized in GCX?

In Biggs and Selfridge [1986], the system included expert knowledge in measures of financial performance, business and the business environment, and management plans. GCX had 100 financial reasoning rules and 80 business and business environment events.

In Selfridge and Biggs [1988a], it was reported that there were six categories of knowledge, including events, inter-event causality, company function (financial model and operations model), events/financial performance causality, measures of financial performance and going concern problems. In that model there were 140 event frames and 215 entity frames.

The model summarized in that paper employs Schank's [1982] MOPs (Memory Organization Packets). For example, in the operations model there is a hierarchy of MOPs that employ successively more detailed descriptions of company operations.

In Selfridge and Biggs [1988b, 1990], that knowledge was extended to general financial knowledge, of actual events, knowledge of normal events, knowledge of company function, knowledge of company markets, knowledge of the industry, knowledge of multiple business lines, knowledge of changes over time and knowledge of other companies.

In each of the successive models the knowledge changes. As a result, the resultant auditor reasoning through that knowledge also must change. That is reflected in each of the papers.

In addition, to addressing the issues specified by the authors, the sequence of papers that reflect the development of GCX allow insight into the growth and development of an expert system.

Dillard and Mutchler [1986, 1987a and 1987b] also have done extensive work in the area of modeling the auditor's going concern opinion decision. Their system was developed on a DEC 2060 using a menu shell, XINFO. The system apparently employs approximately 450 decision frames or nodes in a decision tree. The intelligence in the system is in the decision structure and hierarchy.

The system contains "technical" knowledge about such things as basic accounting procedures, audit procedures, audit standards and the business, economic and legal environment in the context of a "task support system." This knowledge is organized in a hierarchical branching structure with nodes representing primitive and intermediate decisions. Technical knowledge was gathered in each of seven categories: operations, financial, market, management, industry, audit and other.

The system uses an architecture that interfaces that task support system with three other components: task action system, external interface system and a guidance system. The task guidance system uses frames to provide suggestions and, rules and methods for making decisions specified in the task support system. The task action system supports programs for data access, statistical analysis and other additional tools that the auditor may wish to use. Finally, the external interface system allows for the generation of documentation and audit trails.

The system does not exactly mimic expert behavior. For example, the system employs numeric rating systems that it is unlikely auditors use in going concern problems.

INTERNAL CONTROLS

TICOM (Bailey et al. [1985]) was the first auditing-based system to implement artificial intelligence techniques in the system. TICOM (The Internal Control Model) is an analytic tool that aids the auditor in modeling the internal control system and querying the model in order to aid the auditor in evaluating the internal control system. TICOM was implemented in Pascal.

MATERIALITY

Steinbart [1984,1986] developed an audit judgment model, AUDITPLANNER, for the assessment of materiality. AUDITPLANNER uses six different sets of inputs to aid in the materiality decision: prior year's materiality levels, financial characteristics of the client, nonfinancial characteristics of the client, future plans of the client, nature of the audit engagement and the intended uses of the client's financial statements.

The system was built for use in profit and not-for-profit firms. The test clients included manufacturing firms, trucking firms, super markets, a school district and a Boy Scout Council.

AUDITPLANNER was built using the rule-based expert system shell, EMYCIN. The system did not include the use of certainty factors.

RISK ASSESSMENT

Substantial literature of risk assessment exists (e.g., Mock and Vertinsky [1985]). However, there are a number of problems where it is difficult to quantify risk. As a result, Dhar et al. [1988] describe "… the problem of risk assessment as knowledge-based, where knowledge about the client' history, recent events specific to the firm or industry, and knowledge about the internals of a firm are crucial in shaping the auditor's judgment about risks associated with accounts, and hence the audit plan." This interpretation is further enhanced by the general finding (Mock and Vertinsky [1984, p. 1]) that people are "not good intuitive statisticians and therefore the craft of risk assessment is fraught with risks."

There is at least one paper on the use of risk assessment in auditing decision support systems (Mock and Vertinsky [1984]) and at least two papers in the use of expert systems in assessing risk (Dhar et al. [1987] and Peters et al. [1987]).

External Auditing: Commercial-based Systems

ARTHUR ANDERSON

Arthur Anderson (AA) has developed expert systems for the consulting group's clients, e.g., Arthur Anderson [1985] and Mui and McCarthy [1987]. However, there have been no discussions in the literature relating to internal projects to aid the AA auditing process.

ERNST & YOUNG

Ernst & Young (EY) has taken a single product, multiple component, middle-out strategy in the development of their decision support system, EY/ASQ. EY/ASQ is software designed to automate the audit process for manufacturing environments.

EY/ASQ was developed in an Apple MacIntosh environment. The operation for each of the applications is similar to the other applications. The system consists of several modules including Decision Support, Office, Trial Balance, Time Control and Databridge.

The decision support module features the ability to reference the computer file stored documentation for the EY audit process. In addition, the system guides the audit planning process through a "smart questionnaire" approach. This smart questionnaire approach ensures that the auditor performs certain procedures. When those procedures have been followed, the computer updates the rest of the checklist.

Future enhancements likely will include the development of similar modules for different industries and the development of a module to analyze internal controls.

KPMG

KPMG apparently has taken a multiple project approach to the development of expert systems in auditing. Their best known system is Loanprobe, also known as CFILE. The development of that system is chronicled in a sequence of papers, including Kelly, Ribar and Willingham [1987], Ribar [1987, 1988a, 1988b, 1988c]. CFILE is a rule-based system developed using INSIGHT II (now Level V). A rule-based approach is used because of the classification nature of the problem. (Similar classification problems have been solved using a rule-based approach.) It is estimated that CFILE has three person–years of development time (Ribar [1987]).

CFILE derives its name from credit file analysis and is designed for use in bank audits loan loss evaluation. In particular, it aids the process of estimating the dollar amount of the reserve for the bank's portfolio of loans.

AUDPREX (Kelly [1986]) is a proposal to develop an expert system to aid in the design of audit programs in the area of inventory systems. Such a system would be used as an aid to determine the type, timing, nature and the amount of substantive procedures.

In contrast to CFILE, another system, designed to aid in interpretation of SFAS #80 on accounting futures, was done by a single researcher within a period of several weeks (Ribar [1987]). That

23

included the time required by the researcher to learn the expert system shell, INSIGHT II. For the SFAS-based system, the professional literature provided much of the guidance.

Governmental Auditing

Governments face the problem of auditing and reviewing large volumes of tax returns and filings of various types. The large volume often means that humans are unable to process all the documents in a cost - effective manner. Alternatively, even if humans could process all the volume, often budgetary constraints limit the number and quality of persons that could be employed. As a result, the need for systems aimed at processing similar documents submitted to the government is likely to be very high. The successful development of the following systems indicates that such systems may be widespread in the near future.

Each of the following systems has been developed as either a consulting project or as an activity of an internal artificial intelligence staff.

REVIEWS OF SEC FILINGS

Currently, human financial analysts use analytic review of corporate filings at the Securities and Exchange Commission (SEC) to check the correctness of the filings. Arthur Andersen & Co. [1985] (see also Mui and McCarthy [1987]) developed Financial Statement Analyzer (FSA) as a LISP-based prototype to explore the possibility of using a computer program to compute and analyze ratios. FSA includes the ability to "understand" the text in the filings so that it may gather relevant information required to complete an analytic review of the return. Such a system would limit the need for human financial analysts to perform those activities and free their time up for other activities.

From a research perspective, this system is one of the first functioning systems to employ the approach summarized in DeJong [1979] to read and understand natural language. Briefly, that approach reads a part of the sentence. It then predicts what will follow in the remainder of the sentence. Then it checks its prediction against what it actually finds to confirm and guide its search for meaning in the rest of the text. The system continues in this manner, predicting and substantiating while generating its understanding of the text.

PENNSYLVANIA STATE AUDIT FOR TAXES

Green et al. [1990] address the problem of determining "Which Organizations should be audited to achieve the maximum collection of monies due to the state of Pennsylvania?" Accordingly, the overall audit goal is to improve audit productivity.

Unfortunately, this problem is difficult to solve since there is little understanding about which organizations should be audited. Thus, there is little available expertise to build into the system. As a result, Hall et al. [1987] and Greene et al. [1992] developed a system that would learn and develop the necessary expertise.

The general research goal of their paper is to determine how a computer program can be programmed to learn. In order to accomplish that goal they chose a genetic learning approach. Genetic algorithms learn by employing different combining rules on responses, such as inversion and mutation. For example, the system may combine the two sets of characteristics abc and cde to form abe, in its search for a better set of characteristics.

IRS AUDITING OF TAX RETURNS

A recent publication by the Department of the Treasury [1987] indicated that the Internal Revenue Service's new artificial intelligence lab is exploring new systems to identify likely tax returns for examination potential. Very little has been released on their efforts todate, but summaries of activities may be found in Brown [1988], Brown and Strect [1988]. However, they face a problem similar to other government activities, in that they have a number of documents to process in a short time and are subject to budgetary constraints.

DANISH CUSTOMS AUDITING OF VALUE ADDED TAX (VAT) ACCOUNTS

Recently, Danish Customs Authorities employed a consulting firm to develop an expert system to help them audit VAT accounts Lethan and Jacobsen [1987]. The system was designed to develop more effective VAT auditing and to improve the VAT examiner's productivity. As in other government applications, there is a great deal of work to be done and the expert system is designed to do some the work in order to improve the productivity of the examiners.

To acquire the knowledge necessary for the system, the knowledge engineers found that they almost had to become "experts" in the VAT auditing process. Further, for the system to be used by Danish

Customs officers at the sites of the companies that were being investigated the system would have to be developed for use on an IBM-PC and the knowledge base would have to be in Danish. The system was developed using the expert system shell, KEE.

CONTRIBUTIONS AND EXTENSIONS OF GOVERNMENT AUDIT SYSTEMS

Each of these systems is important because they capture the knowledge of experts in their knowledge bases and allow for productivity improvements. Each of these systems is designed to allow computer processing of some human information processing activities, while allowing humans to focus on other more important issues.

However, there are additional contributions. The FSA was one of the first actual implementations of DeJong's [1979] approach to understanding text. The Pennsylvania State Tax system is the first audit system to be able to learn. The VAT system demonstrates an easy to forget capability of expert systems that the knowledge does not have to be recorded in English—the system does not care what language the knowledge is in.

Systems of this type are not limited to these applications. Instead, those situations where there are a large number of documents to process and those situations where there is interest in determining file violations are all conceptually congruent with these applications. In addition, although each of these applications is associated with a government, such applications are not limited to government but could be extended to almost any business that processes large amounts of the same kind of documents.

Internal Auditing

The functional area of auditing that probably has received the least attention is internal auditing. Although internal auditors will likely make use of many of the developments in each of the other categories discussed above, some applications have been aimed at the unique requirements of internal auditing.

DECISION SUPPORT FOR INTERNAL AUDIT PLANNING

Boritz [1983] presented an initial report on the development of a desktop decision support system for internal auditing planning. That system (Boritz [1986-a]) is available to the commercial market through the Institute of Internal Auditors (IIA) as a product known as "audit MASTERPLAN" (AMP).

26

AMP includes two approaches to measuring risk (Based on Boritz [1986-b]) and includes the IIA's Standards for Professional Practice of Internal Auditing. AMP is designed for most industries (financial, industrial, service and manufacturing). AMP has five components: Systems Management, Risk Factors Management, Audit Portfolio Management, Personnel Skills Management and Long-term Planning and Budgeting Module.

In the original report (Boritz [1983]), the research focus was on the user interface and the inclusion of knowledge into the procedures of the system rather than the storage of a separate knowledge base. Boritz and Kielstra [1987] described a methodology for the assessment of risk, using audit and inherent risk.

PRICE ANALYSIS

A problem that continues to make headlines throughout the country is the spending activities of the federal government, e.g., the two hundred dollar ashtray. In a sequence of at least three papers Dillard et al. [1983,1987] and Ramakrishna et al. [1983] proposed the development of an expert system to aid in the examination of the reasonableness of an expenditure.

Their discussion was primarily aimed at federal government acquisitions. However, as they note, price analysis is also a problem in private enterprise.

PAYPER—AN EXPERT SYSTEM TO EXAMINE PAYROLL AND PERSONNEL FILES

Payper (Payroll–Personnel) is a prototype expert system, developed using the expert system shell EXSYS, designed to aid in the audit of payroll and personnel files. It does this by ensuring that conditions within each field of each record meet certain conditions and that the analytical relationships that hold between fields meet certain conditions. For example, not only should hours worked and pay rate meet certain constraints, but also hours worked times pay rate plus vacation pay must meet certain constraints.

The primary theoretical contribution of PAYPER is that it uses traditional expert systems, multiple conditions rules, to extend traditional EDP audit tests. By taking into account relations between the fields, this approach allows tighter and more comprehensive analysis of the data. In addition, it allows investigation of text data in such audit processes.

THE INTERNAL AUDIT RISK ASSESSOR (TIARA)— THE EQUITABLE

There is only limited information available on TIARA as developed by Inference Corporation for The Equitable. A brief summary of the system is available (Inference Corp–No Date) and further inquiries to Inference Corporation did not yield any additional information, except that the system was not used by The Equitable.

As originally discussed TIARA presents a methodology for assessing risk. Some of the variables used in that decision include strength/experience of the units management team, the unit's internal control consciousness, changes in the unit's basic industry/market and the length of time since their last audit. The system was designed to provide a means to enable rapid identification of high priority audits and consistent assessment of audit risk.

COOPERS & LYBRAND—INTERNAL AUDIT SYSTEMS

Coopers & Lybrand have devolped a general internal audit system that

- Employs Audit Planning and Tracking
- Allows Automatic Sample Selection from Mainframe Data
- Automatically identifies Patterns in Sample Data
- Has Intelligent online questionnaires for policy testing and specific regulation
- Provides explanations for questions
- Records internal auditor comments during the audit
- Displays policy documents online
- Generates Work Papers
- Prints branch exception reports

CONTINUOUS AUDIT OF ONLINE SYSTEMS

Vasarhelyi et al. [1988] argue that recent advances in hardware and software technology are engendering increasingly complex information systems environments, thus, requiring increasingly complex audit approaches. However, the same technologies that increase the complexity of the information systems environment can be used to the advantage of the auditing those systems. Not only can decision support systems be used to assist auditors, but the computer can be used to perform additional auditing. In particular, because of the large amount of data, auditors may not be able to provide an effective or efficient audit. As a result, it is desirable to build systems that continuously audit portions of the database as transactions occur.

The quality of these audit systems is dependent on the ability of the modeler to capture the expertise of auditors in the metrics and analytics used to model that expertise. Research in systems of this type needs to explore approaches that capture that expertise best.

FRAUD DETECTION

At least two studies (Tener [1988] and Lecot [1988]) have used expert systems to investigate the possibility of fraud as part of the internal audit function.

Tener [1988] discusses an off-line fraud detection system for deviant file use. Lecot [1988] describes an on-line system designed to determine fraudulent credit card use. In each case the focus of these systems was on determining if a user of a service of the firm is a legitimate user. Conceptually, the intrusion detection systems discussed under EDP systems and the continuous audit system discussed immediately above are similar to these systems.

The approach of each system is to first establish a profile for each of the legitimate users, that defines expected and possible behaviors. Then when that user makes use of the system, that use is compared to the profile to determine if the user is who they say they are. Those comparisons are based on the notion that "early warning symptoms" can be captured in those user profiles.

Tener [1986] suggests that audit management utilize decision support systems, management information systems and management science models to identify and project the deterioration of controls that can occur between audit engagements. Further, as firms increase in size, because of mergers and economies of scale, the quantity of auditing demands on the auditor is increasing.

Dangers in Expert System Development

One of the dangers of the current approach to most knowledge engineering projects is the preoccupation with what is, rather than what should be.

In other words, sometimes one gets "caught up" in the method or technology without considering other options, approaches, methods or "old" technologies for solving problems. For example, on one expert system project of which the authors are aware, the knowledge engineer was attempting to fit "everything" into a rule-based expert system; it was then suggested that a mathematical programming approach (integer programming) would provide a better solution to a subproblem in the system than using a sequence of if-then rules. The linear program was able to provide a better solution than simply mimicking an auditor's behavior. When optimal solution generation processes can be used to solve the problem they will provide better solutions than rule-based approaches.

Preoccupation with a given type of knowledge representation can be dangerous. For example, as Biggs et al. [1986] found auditors do not think in "If ... then ... " rules. Turning dialogues with auditors into such rules may lead to a loss of knowledge.

In a related study, Gal and Steinbart [1986] examined the development of two expert systems for investigating the nature of audit judgment. The evidence presented in that paper indicates that "refinements made to those prototype systems resulted in evaluations which reflect more of the decision criteria actually used by the auditor." That is, the initial systems developed may not properly represent judgment.

Another danger in the development of expert systems is that the more computers do the less auditors need to do. This has at least two implications. First, we must remember that expert systems are a move to automate the audit process. As with the introduction of most automation projects, the number of human workers directly involved in the production process decreases. Thus, we can expect to see a decrease in the number of auditors to accomplish the same amount of work. Second, if the system knows something then the auditor may not need to know that something. As a result, auditors may forget important information that they have learned or not learn things that are important. Reportedly, EY has tempered the inclusion of activities in EY/ASQ so as to minimize the negative implications of the system knowing "too much," and the auditor forgetting or worse yet, not learning.

Another danger is that the auditor would blindly depend on the systems' recommendations. This could occur in at least two situations. First, if the auditor does not have the necessary base knowledge then decisions made by the system cannot be questioned. Second, if the auditor does not "interact" with the systems then the systems suggested course of action will be executed. As a result, it is important to place the responsibility for the actions on the auditor, not the system.

Further, there are security problems associated with expert systems that are different than those associated with other computer-based systems. Such security problems are discussed in O'Leary [1990].

VALIDATING EXPERT SYSTEMS

Recently, there has been considerable interest in validating expert systems. O'Leary [1987] provided a framework for validation of expert systems. That framework is particularly useful because it elicits some of the key issues and concerns that face the validator of an expert system. Particular methods for validating expert systems are investigated and developed in O'Leary [1988b], O'Leary and Kandelin [1988] and others.

Continued development in this area is expected so that tools are developed to meet the needs of validators. Many of these issues and other issues are summarized in O'Leary [1993].

Conclusions

Recently developed audit-based expert systems have moved beyond the initial rule-based systems to include such knowledge representation schemas as frames and semantic networks. The systems went beyond just employing heuristics in the context of decision making processes, to include developments, such as learning and natural language understanding. In addition, expert systems have moved out of academe and into commercial applications.

As summarized in this paper, a wide variety of prototype and commercial systems are in operation. Thus, from an academic perspective there is no more need to build expert systems to show that they can be used to solve accounting problems.

However, expert systems remain an important tool to simulate the procedures that an auditor goes through, to test our understanding of the knowledge in a particular area of auditing and to test the use of technological developments in artificial intelligence in auditing-based expert systems.

Prior Surveys on Expert Systems in Accounting, Auditing and Related Areas

The review of the literature also meant investigating any previous surveys of various groups, e.g. CPA firms, to determine what those surveys found. No surveys were found. However, since the survey of internal auditors summarized in this report was made, two other surveys have been completed.

Previous Surveys on the Use of Expert Systems

Only limited survey research has been done on the use of expert systems in financial and accounting applications. The purpose of this section is to discuss two of those studies.

SURVEY OF SMALL AND MEDIUM SIZED CPA FIRMS

Barbera [1988] surveyed 148 local New York CPA firms to determine, among other things the extent of their knowledge, use and interest in expert systems and artificial intelligence. After three mailings only 28 out of 148 (19%) firms responded to the survey. This suggests at best limited interest in the expert systems and artificial intelligence.

The responses to the survey indicated that expert systems software was not used by any of the firms. However, 53% knew what expert systems were and 46% of the firms were aware of possible expert system uses. 20% of the firms said they were monitoring possible expert system use by the firm and 18% said that they were contemplating use.

Only 9 of the 28 respondents (6% of the 148 firms) replied to a portion of the survey that related to possible applications of expert systems. Four of the nine (44%) respondents indicated that expert systems were inappropriate for education/training and diagnosis. Since these areas are among the most frequently referenced "successes" for expert systems and since there is such a small sample of respondents some question exists as to the end use of the results reported in this study.

SURVEY OF FINANCIAL SERVICES FIRMS

In 1987, Coopers & Lybrand [1988a, 1988b, 1988c] surveyed 90 of the largest U.S. financial services institutions. These institutions include commercial banks, security firms, insurance companies, thrifts and investment companies. The comments that follow have not been made with the advantage of having seen the primary report of survey statistics—most of which apparently are in Coopers & Lybrand [1988c]. However, heavy use of Coopers & Lybrand [1988a and 1988b] are made.

LEVELS OF ACTIVITY

The survey found that 60% of the commercial banks, over 50% of the security firms, just over 40% of the insurance companies and virtually none of the thrifts and investment companies were either researching, developing or using expert systems. One third of the firms that had not yet started to develop an expert system, expected to do so by 1990.

Further, the survey (Coopers & Lybrand [1988a, 1988b]) found "... that 53% of the firms surveyed have applications that use expert systems, are in the process of developing such systems or are planning for them." In particular, the survey found that 12% were using, 31% were developing and 10% were planning expert systems. These percentages are not unexpected, particularly since financial institutions traditionally have used data processing applications to increase productivity and reduce costs.

STRATEGIC IMPORTANCE AND BENEFITS

90% of the respondents who already have an expert system in use, 93% of those developing an expert system and 77% of those planning an expert system believe that the technology is a competitive necessity. The overall benefits to be derived from expert systems cited by the respondents include increased profits, broader distribution of scarce resources and higher quality and more consistency of employees. Those benefits are summarized in Table 3-1.

APPLICATIONS

The survey found almost 55 expert systems being developed, evaluated or being used. The applications differed across the financial industry, based on industry segment. The primary applications are summarized in Table 3-2.

RESPONSIBILITY FOR DEVELOPMENT

The survey found that currently almost 75% of all expert systems activity in the financial services industry involves both the end user department and the data processing department. However, over the next three to five years the companies surveyed expect a movement toward end user based systems.

Table 3-1

BENEFITS OF EXPERT SYSTEMS AS REPORTED BY
RESPONDENTS[1]

Benefit	% of Respondents with Expert Systems in Use	% of Respondents Currently Developing Expert Systems
Increased Profits	56	15
Broader Distribution of Scarce Resources	33	14
Improved Quality/Consistency of Employee Output	22	7
Improved Training	11	14
Increased Experience With Expert Systems	11	29
No Benefits Derived Yet	22	57

[1] *Source: Coopers & Lybrand [1988a]*

DEVELOPMENT ENVIRONMENT

Over 50% of the respondents developed expert systems using an expert system shell, augmented by custom programming. 33% used a shell exclusively and only 10% of the respondents did not use a commercial shell.

Although respondents indicated that about 33% of the applications had been developed using LISP work stations, they also indicated that they will dramatically reduce their use of LISP for development and delivery. Instead, they indicate that they prefer PC's and mainframes.

WHO IS DOING THE DEVELOPMENT

50% of those companies actively pursuing expert systems use both

Table 3-2

PRIMARY APPLICATIONS—BY INDUSTRY

Banks
    Loan Processing (55 expert systems are being evaluated,
        developed or used)
    Business Loan Processing
    Consumer Loan Processing
    Mortgage Loan Processing
    Trading (Over 40 are being used or developed)

Securities Industry
    Trading (6 in use and 13 being evaluated or developed)
    Trading Risk Assessment
    Stock Option Trading

Investment Companies
    Portfolio Management
    Securities Selection

Source: Coopers & Lybrand [1988a]

internal personnel and external developers to produce the system. However, 40% are using only their firm's personnel. Slightly over 33% report that end-user groups are responsible for the maintenance of the knowledge base.

OBSTACLES

Top management may be skeptical of ES and therefore may not provide the necessary support. Participants reported that 34% of their top management believe that expert systems are necessary for competitive positioning. 53% believe it is too early for their companies to be able to assess the need for expert systems. Thus, the respondents believe that the most important future development in expert systems technology will be a track record of success stories in the industry. The availability of software on conventional hardware and connectivity between expert systems and databases are perceived as major difficulties. Those with expert systems suggested that the complexity of existing expert systems tools is a major difficulty. Surprisingly, cost was not found to be a major deferent to expert system use. The relative importance of various reasons is summarized in Table 3-3.

```
┌─────────────────────────────────────────────────────┐
│                     Table 3-3                         │
│                                                       │
│              OBSTACLES TO DEVELOPMENT                  │
│  ─────────────────────────────────────────────────   │
│                                                       │
│  1. Track Record of Success                           │
│  2. Conventional Hardware for Expert Systems          │
│  3. Connectivity of AI Hardware and Software          │
│  4. Ease of Use                                       │
│  5. "Off the Shelf" Availability                      │
│  6. Easier to Identify Applications                   │
│  7. Lower Cost of Delivery                            │
│  8. Availability of Knowledge Engineers               │
│  9. Lower Cost of Development                          │
│                                                       │
│  *Source Coopers & Lybrand*                           │
└─────────────────────────────────────────────────────┘
```

References

AICPA, Statements on Auditing Standards, #59, "The Auditor' Consideration of an Entity's Ability to Continue as a Going Concern," 1988.

Amer, T., Bailey, A., and De, P., "A Review of Computer Information Systems Research Related to Accounting and Auditing," The Journal of Accounting Information Systems, Volume Two, Number One, Fall 1987, pp. 3-28.

Arthur Andersen & Co., Financial Statement Analyzer, Unpublished report, December 1985.

Ashby, R., Introduction to Cybernetics, John Wiley & Sons, 1965

Bailey, A., Meservy, R., Duke, G., Johnson, P. and Thompson, W., "Auditing, Artificial Intelligence and Expert Systems," Decision Support Systems: Theory and Applications, Edited by C. Holsapple and A. Whinston, Springer Verlagg, Berlin, 1987.

Bailey, A.D., Duke, G.L., Gerlach, J., Ko, C., Meservy, R.D., Whinston, A.B., "TICOM and the Analysis of Internal Controls," The Accounting Review, 60, April, 1985, pp. 186-201.

————, Meservy, R., and Turner, J., "Decision Support Systems, Expert Systems, and Artificial Intelligence: Realities and Possibilities in Public Accounting," The Ohio CPA Journal, Spring, 1986, pp. 11-15.

Barbera, A., "Personal Computer and Expert System Usage by Small and Medium Sized CPA Firms," Unpublished paper, July, 1988.

Bedard, J., Gray, G. and Mock, T.J., "Decision Support Systems and Auditing," Advances in Accounting, B. Schwartz (ed), JAI Press, Greenwich, Connecticut, 1984.

Biggs, S., Messier, W. and Hansen, J., "A Descriptive Analysis of Computer Audit Specialists' Decision-Making Behavior in Advanced Computer Environments," Auditing: A Journal of Theory and Practice, Spring 1987, Volume 6 Number 2, pp. 1-21

———— and Selfridge, M. "GCX: An Expert System for the Auditor's Going Concern Judgment," Unpublished presentation at the National Meeting of the American Accounting Association in New York, 1986.

Blocher, E., Krull, G., Scalf, K. and Yates, S., "Training and Performance Effects of A Knowledge-Based System for Analytical Review," Unpublished Paper Presented at the First International Symposium on Expert Systems in Business, Finance and Accounting, University of Southern California, September 1988.

Bolc and Coombs, Expert Systems Applications, Springer-Verlagg, New York, 1988.

Boritz, J., "CAPS: The Comprehensive Audit Planning System," Unpublished Paper presented at the University of Southern California Symposium on Audit Judgment, 1983.

————, "Audit MASTERPLAN," Audit Planning Software published by the Institute of Internal Auditors, 1986-a.

————, "Scheduling Internal Audit Activities," Auditing: A Journal of Theory and Practice, Fall 1986-b, Volume 6, Number 1, pp. 1-19.

———— and Kielstra, R., "A Prototype Expert System for the Assessment of Inherent Risk and Prior Probability of Error," Unpublished Paper, 1987.

————. and Wensley, A., "Structuring the Assessment of Audit Evidence - An Expert Systems Approach," December 1987, Unpublished Paper.

Borthick, F., "Artificial Intelligence in Auditing: Assumptions and Preliminary Development," Advances in Accounting, 1987a, pp. 179-204.

―――― and West, O., "Expert Systems—A New Tool for The Professional," Accounting Horizons, March, 1987b, Volume One, Number One, pp. 9-16.

Braun, H.M., "Integrating an Expert System and Analytical Review Techniques for Making an Audit Decision," Unpublished paper presented at the ORSA/TIMS meeting in Miami, October, 1986.

Brown, C. and Streit, I., "A Survey of Tax Expert Systems," Expert Systems Review, Volume I, Number 2, 1988, pp. 6-12.

Buchanan, B.G. and Shortliffe, E.H., Rule-Based Expert Systems, Addison -Wesley, Reading, Massachusetts, 1984.

Bull, M., et. al., "Applying Software Engineering Principles to Knowledge Base Development," Proceedings of the First Annual Conference on Expert Systems in Business, New York, NY, November 1987, pp. 27-38.

Chandler, J., "Expert Systems in Auditing: The State of the Art," The Auditor's Report, Volume 8, Number 3, Summer 1985, pp. 1-4.

Chandler, J., Braun, H. and Dungan, C., "Expert Systems: Operational Support for Audit Decision Making," Unpublished paper presented at the University of Southern California Symposium on Audit Judgment, February 1983.

Coopers & Lybrand, "Expert Systems Catching On With Financial Services Firms," Executive Briefing, May 1988a.

―――――, Expert Systems in the Financial Services Industry, Coopers & Lybrand 1988b.

―――――, Expert Systems in the Financial Services Industry: Survey Report, Coopers & Lybrand 1988c (Cost is $100).

Davis, D., "Artificial Intelligence Goes to Work," High Technology, April 1987.

Denning, D., "An Intrusion Detection Model," IEEE Transactions on Software Engineering, Vol. SE 13, No. 2, February 1987, pp. 222-232.

―――――, "An Intrusion Detection Model," IEEE Transactions on Software Engineering, Vol SE 14, No. 3, March 1987, pp. 252-261.

————, et. al, "Views for Multilevel Databases," IEEE Transactions on Software Engineering, Vol. SE 13, No. 2, February 1987, pp. 129-139.

Dhar, V., Lewis, B., and Peters, J., "A Knowledge-Based Model of Audit Risk," AI Magazine, Volume 9, Number 3, Fall 1988.

DeJong, G., Skimming Stories in Real Time: An experiment in Integrated Understanding, Unpublished Ph. D. Dissertation, Yale University, 1979.

Dillard, J., "Discussant's Comments on 'Expert Systems in Accounting and Auditing: A Framework and Review'" Decision Making and Accounting: Current Research, S. Moriarty and E. Joyce (beds.), University of Oklahoma, 1984, pp. 182-202.

———— and Mutchler, J.F., "Knowledge Based Expert Systems in Auditing," Working Paper, Ohio State University, July, 1984.

———— and ————, "Knowledge Based Expert Computer Systems for Audit Opinion Decisions," Unpublished Paper presented at the University of Southern California Symposium on Audit Judgment, 1986.

———— and ————, "A Knowledge-Based Support System for the Auditor's Going Concern Opinion Decision," Unpublished Working Paper, 1987a.

———— and ————, "Expertise in Assessing Solvency Problems," Expert Systems, August 1987b, pp. 170-178.

————, Ramakrishna, K. and Chandrasekaran, B., "Expert Systems for Price Analysis: A Feasibility Study," in Federal Acquisition Research Symposium, U.S. Air Force, Williamsburg, Virginia, December, 1983.

————, ———— and ————, "Knowledge-based Decision Support Systems for Military Procurement," in Silverman [1987], pp. 120-139.

Dungan, C. "A Model of an Audit Judgement in the Form of an Expert System," University of Illinois, Unpublished Ph.D. Dissertation, (1983).

———— and Chandler, J., "Analysis of Audit Judgment Through an Expert System," Faculty Working Paper no. 982, University of Illinois, November, 1983.

—— and ——, "Auditor: A Microcomputer-Based Expert System to Support Auditors in the Field," Expert Systems, October, 1985, pp. 210-221.

Elliot, R.K. and Kielich, J.A., "Expert Systems for Accountants," Journal of Accountancy, September, 1985.

Flesher, D. and Martin, C., "Artificial Intelligence," The Internal Auditor, February, 1987, pp. 32-36.

Fox, M., "Artificial Intelligence in Knowledge Representation," Proceedings of the Sixth International Joint Conference on Artificial Intelligence, Volume 1, Morgan Kaufmann, Palo Alto, CA 1979, pp. 282-284.

Gal, G., "Using Auditor Knowledge to Formulate Data Constraints: An Expert System for Internal Control Evaluation," Unpublished Ph. D. Dissertation, Michigan State University, 1985.

—— and Steinbart, P., "Knowledge Base Refinements as an Indication of Auditor Experience," Unpublished paper presented at the University of Southern California Symposium on Audit Judgment, 1986.

Gerlach, J., "Some Preliminary Notes on the Development of a General DSS for Auditors," Decision Support Systems: Theory and Application, Edited by C. Holsapple and A. Whinston, Springer Verlag, Berlin, 1987.

Greene, D., Meservy, R. and Smith, S., "Learning Audit Selection Rules From Data," in O'Leary, D. and Watkins, P., Expert Systems in Finance, North-Holland, Amsterdam, 1992.

Grudnitski, G., "A Prototype of an Internal Control System for the Sales/Accounts Receivable Application," Unpublished paper presented at the University of Southern California Symposium on Audit Judgment, 1986.

Hall, M., Meservy, R. and Nagin, D., "Audit Knowledge Acquisition by Computer Learning." Unpublished paper presented at the ORSA/TIMS Meeting, New Orleans, May, 1987.

Halper, S., Davis, G., O'Neil-Dunne, P.J., and Pfau, P., Handbook of EDP Auditing, Warren, Gorham & Lamont, Boston, 1985.

Hansen, J.V. and Messier, W.F., "Expert Systems for Decision Support in EDP Auditing," International Journal of Computer and Information Sciences, 11, (1982), pp. 357-379.

———— and ————, "A Knowledge-Based Expert System for Auditing Advanced Computer Systems," European Journal of Operational Research, September 1986a, pp. 371-379.

———— and ————, "A Preliminary Investigation of EDP-XPERT," Auditing: A Journal of Practice and Theory, Volume 6, Number 1,Fall, 1986b, pp. 109-123.

Hayes-Roth, F., Waterman, D.A., Lenat, D.B., Building Expert Systems, Addison-Wesley, Reading, Massachusetts, 1983.

Hogarth, R., Judgment and Choice, Wiley, Chichester, 1985.

Holsapple, C. and Whinston, A., Business Expert Systems, Irwin, Homewood, Illinois, 1987.

Holstrom, G., "Sources of Error and Inconsistency in Audit Judgment," Working paper no. 70, School of Accounting, University of Southern California, 1984.

Holstrom, G., Mock, T. and West, R., "The Impact of Technological Events and Trends on Audit Evidence in the Year 2000: Phase I," in Proceedings of the 1986 Touche Ross / University of Kansas Symposium on Auditing Problems, edited by Srivastava, R. and Ford, N., School of Business, University of Kansas, Lawerence, Kansas 66045, 1987, pp. 125-146.

Inference Corporation, "The Internal Audit Risk Assessor (TIARA) - The Equitable," ART Application Note, Inference Corporation, Los Angeles, California

Jamieson, R., "Auditing Knowledge Based Systems," Monograph for EDP Auditors Foundation, Australia, University of New South Wales, January 1990.

Kelly, K.P., Expert Problem Solving for the Audit Planning Process, Unpublished Ph. D. Dissertation, University of Pittsburgh, Pittsburgh, Pa., 1984.

————, "Audit Programming Expert System Project," Unpublished paper, 1986.

————, "Modeling the Audit Planning Process," Expert Systems Review, Volume 1, Number 1, 1987.

————, Ribar, G. and Willingham, J., "Interim Report on the Development of an Expert System for the Auditors Loan Loss Evaluation," in Proceedings of the Touche Ross/University of Kansas Audit Symposium, 1987, pp. 167-188.

Kick, R., "Auditing an Expert System," Expert Systems, Summer 1989, pp. 33-38.

Kolodner, J., Retrieval and Organizational Strategies in Conceptual Memory: A Computer Memory, Unpublished Ph. D. Dissertation, Yale University, 1980.

Lecot, K., "An Expert System Approach to Fraud Prevention and Detection," AI-88 Artificial Intelligence Conference, Long Beach, Ca.

———, "An Expert System Approach to Fraud Prevention and Detection," Expert Systems Review, Volume 1, Number 3, 1988.

Lethan, H. and Jacobsen, H., "ESKORT—An Expert System for Auditing VAT Accounts," in Proceedings of Expert Systems and Their Applications—Avignon 87," Avignon, France, 1987.

Lewis, B. and Dhar, V., "Development of a Knowledge-based Expert System for Auditing," Unpublished Research Proposal, University of Pittsburgh, 1985.

McKee, T., "Expert Systems: The Final Frontier?," The CPA Journal, July, 1986, pp. 42-46.

Meservy, R.D., "Auditing Internal Controls: A Computational Model of the Review Process," Unpublished Dissertation Proposal, University of Minnesota, October, 1984.

———, Bailey, A. and Johnson, P., "Internal Control Evaluation: A Computational Model of the Review Process," Auditing: A Journal of Theory and Practice, Volume 6, Number 1, Fall 1986, pp. 44-74.

Messier, W.F. and Hansen, J.V., "Expert Systems in Auditing: A Framework and Review," Decision Making and Accounting: Current Research, S. Moriarty and E. Joyce (eds.), University of Oklahoma, 1984, pp. 182-202.

Messier, W.F. and Hansen, J.V., "A Case Study and Field Evaluation of EDP-EXPERT", International Journal of Intelligent Systems in Accounting, Finance and Management, Volume 1, Number 4, pp. 173-185, 1992.

Michaelsen, R., A Knowledge-based System for Individual Income and Transfer Tax Planning, University of Illinois, 1991.

Mock, T. and Vertinsky, I., "DSS-RAA: Design Highlights," Unpublished Paper Presented at the University of Southern California Audit Judgment Conference, February 1984.

—— and ——, Risk Assessment in Accounting and Auditing, Research Monograph Number 10, The Canadian Certified General Accountants Research Foundation, Vancouver, British Columbia, Canada, 1985.

Moeller, R., Artificial Intelligence—A Primer, Institute of Internal Auditors Monograph Series, 1987.

——, "Expert Systems: Auditability Issues," Unpublished paper presented at the First International Symposium for Expert Systems in Business, Finance and Accounting, October 1988. Forthcoming in Expert Systems in Business and Finance, John Wiley, 1991.

Mui, C. and McCarthy, W., FSA: Applying AI Techniques to the Familiarization Phase of Financial Decision Making," IEEE Expert, Vol. 2, No. 3, 1987, pp. 33-41.

Nazareth, D., "Issues in the Verification of Knowledge in Rule-based Systems," International Journal of Man-Machine Studies, Vol 30, pp. 255-271, 1989.

Nyguyen, T., Perkins, W., and Lafferty, T., and Pecora, D., "Knowledge-based Verification," AI Magazine, Volume 8, No. 2, 1987.

O'Leary, D., "Expert Systems in a Personal Computer Environment," Georgia Journal of Accounting, Volume Seven, Spring, 1986, pp. 107-118.

——, "The Use of Artificial Intelligence in Accounting," in Silverman [1987a].

——, "Validation of Expert Systems: With Applications to Accounting and Auditing," Decision Sciences, Volume 17, Number 3, pp. 468-486, 1987.

——, "Expert Systems Prototyping as a Research Tool," in E. Turban and P. Watkins, Applied Expert Systems, North-Holland, 1988a.

——, "Methods of Validating Expert Systems," Interfaces, September-October 1988b.

——, "Security in Expert Systems," IEEE Expert, June 1990, pp. 59-70.

——, "Software Engineering and Research Issues in Accounting Information Systems," Journal of Information Systems, Vol. 2, No. 2, Spring 1988.

————, "Validating and Assessing Expert Systems," Paper presented at the First International Symposium on Expert Systems in Business, Finance and Accounting, University of Southern California, September 1988, to appear in Watkins and Eliot [1993].

————, "Soliciting Weights or Probabilities from Experts for Rule-Based Expert Systems," International Journal of Man-Machine Studies, Vol. 32, pp. 293-301, 1990a.

————, "Verification of Frames and Semantic Network Knowledge Bases," in Preproceedings of the 5th Knowledge Acquisition for Knowledge-based Systems Workshop, Banff Canada, November 1990.

———— and Kandelin, N., "Validating the Weights in Rule-Based Expert Systems," International Journal of Expert Systems: Research and Applications, Volume 1, Number 4, 1988.

———— and Tan, M., "A Knowledge-Based System for Auditing Payroll –Personnel Files," Unpublished Paper, University of Southern California, February, 1987.

———— and Watkins, P., "Review of Expert Systems in Auditing," Expert Systems Review, Volume 2, Numbers 1 and 2, 1989.

Peat, Marwick, Mitchell & Co., Peat Marwick Foundation Research Opportunities in Auditing Program, Interim Report, 1986.

Peters, J., Lewis, B. and Dhar, V., "Assessing Inherent Risk During Audit Planning: A Computational Model," Unpublished Paper, University of Oregon, March 1988.

Ramakrishna, K., Dillard, J.F., Harrison, T.G., and Chandrasekaran, B., "An Intelligent Manual for Price Analysis," in Federal Acquisition Research Symposium, U.S. Air Force, Williamsburg, Virginia, December, 1983.

Ribar, G., "Uses of Expert Systems Technology at Peat Marwick Main," Expert Systems Review, Volume 1, Number 1, 1987.

————, "Development of an Expert System", Expert Systems Review, Volume 1, Number 3, 1988a.

————, "Expert Systems Validation: A Case Study", Expert Systems Review, Volume 1, Number 3, 1988b.

Sauers, R., "Controlling Expert Systems," in Expert Systems Applications, in Bolc and Coombs [1988].

Selfridge, M., "Mental Models and Memory: Expert Systems and Auditing in the Year 2000," Unpublished paper presented at the USC Audit Judgment Conference, February 1988.

—— and Biggs, S., "GCX, A Computational Model of the Auditor's Going Concern Judgment," Unpublished paper presented at the Audit Judgment Symposium, University of Southern California, February 1988a.

—— and ——, "GCX: Knowledge Structures for Going Concern Structures for Going Concern Evaluations," Unpublished Paper presented at the First International Symposium on Expert Systems in Business, Finance and Accounting, University of Southern California, September 1988b.

—— and ——, "The Architecture of Expertise: The Auditor Going Concern Judgement," Expert Systems Review, Volume 2, Number 3, 1990.

Shatz, H., Strahs, R., and Campbell, L., "Expertax: the Issue of Long-Term Maintenance," Proceedings of the Third Internatioal Conference on Expert Systems, Learned Information, Woodside, Hinksey Hill, Oxford England, June 1987, pp. 291-300.

Silverman, B. (ed.), Expert Systems for Business, Addison-Wesley, Reading, Massachusetts, 1987.

Socha, W., "Problems in Auditing Expert System Development," EDPACS, March 1988, pp. 1-6.

Steinbart, P., The Construction of an Expert System to Make Materiality Judgments, Unpublished Ph. D. Dissertation, Michigan State University, 1984.

——, "The Construction of a Rule-based Expert System as a Method for Studying Materiality Judgments," Accounting Review, January 1987.

Tener, W., "Detection of Control Deterioration Using Decision Support Systems," Computers and Security, Vol. 5, 1986, pp. 290-295.

——, "Expert Systems for Computer Security," Expert Systems Review, Vol. 1, No. 2, 1988.

Turban, E., Decision Support and Expert Systems, Macmillan, New York, 1988.

—— and Watkins, P., "Integrating Expert Systems and Decision Support Systems," Management Information Systems Quarterly, June 1986, pp. 121-138.

Turban, E. and Watkins, P., Applied Expert Systems, North-Holland, Amsterdam, 1988.

Vasarhelyi, M., Halper, F., and Fritz, R., "The Continuous Audit of Online Systems," Unpublished Paper presented at the University of Southern California Audit Judgment Conference and the National Meeting of the American Accounting Association, 1988.

Watkins, P. and Eliot, L., Expert Systems in Business and Finance, John Wiley & Co., 1993.

Watne, D. and Turney, P., Auditing EDP Systems, Prentice-Hall, Englewood Cliffs, New Jersey, 1990, pp. 555-590.

Weber, R., EDP Auditing, McGraw-Hill, New York, 1988.

Chapter 4

INTERVIEWS WITH FIRMS USING/DEVELOPING EXPERT SYSTEMS

Interviews were conducted with a number of internal auditors from firms identified as either using expert systems, developing expert systems or investigating the use of expert systems. Interviews were conducted with the internal audit department head or head EDP auditor. Throughout the interviews, the participants were extremely cooperative.

The interviews were accomplished using open ended questions. Because the current use of expert systems is a somewhat nebulous decision making area, it was decided that, particularly at the interview stage, the use of simple "yes-no" like questions would not be beneficial. Much of the open-ended discussion resulted in questions for the survey, discussed in Chapter 9. To maintain as unobtrusive a presence as possible, a formal printed set of questions was not the focus of the interview. Instead, tailoring to the particular firm and internal auditors was the primary concern.

Each interview led to a number of different questions, and some of those questions were incorporated in later interviews. However, the base questions are summarized below. Not all questions were answered fully by each set of internal auditors, often because the questions were not fully applicable to each firm or because of confidentiality or for other reasons.

In addition, the discussion of systems at each firm was limited to those characteristics thought to be most insightful, interesting and different from the interviews with other firms.

Base Interview Questions

• *Type of Applications*
  What is the nature of current applications?
  What types of applications are planned for the future?

• *Detection of Fraud*
  To what extent are ES/AI being used/planned for the detection/
  prevention of fraud?

• *Criteria for Development*
  Describe the cost and benefits issues
  What are the driving forces behind ES/AI activity?
  What constitutes the motivation for pursuing ES/AI within inter-
  nal audit?
  What other uses are anticipated for ES/AI?

• *Maintenance and Continuing Develop-ment of Systems*
  How is maintenance of ES/AI being addressed?
  Are there unique aspects of maintaining and continuing develop-
  ment of ES/AI?

• *Development Environment*
  Who did the development?
  Where did the resources for the development come from?
  Where was the project initiated?
  Mainframe or personal computer?
  Across organization boundaries?
  Integrated into other applications?

• *Problems with Expert Systems*
  Describe any problems or challenges with ES you have developed
  or are currently developing?

• *Auditing of the System*
  To what extent have you provided for the auditing of the ES that
  you have developed or are currently developing?
  Have you developed audit standards and audit plans for ES?

• *Organizational Issues*
  Describe any organizational issues that may have arisen due to
  your involvement with ES utilization/development?
  What future organizational issues do you anticipate with greater
  emphasis on ES/AI within internal auditing?

Overview and Synthesis of Interview Results

Eleven firms participated in the interview phase of the study. These included:

an information services company,
a retail industry chain,
a Fortune 100 manufacturing firm,
a Fortune 100 computer firm,
a large West coast bank,
a stock brokerage firm,
a large international accounting firm (interviewed about a client's brokerage ES),
a large insurance company,
two large East coast banks,
a large aerospace firm.

Although the interview results are somewhat unique and tailored to the specific firms, some general findings can be identified. These findings relate to application areas, project design and development, motivation for ES development, delivery environment (hardware and software), and other benefits, expectations.

APPLICATIONS

In general, most applications were specifically related to internal audit activities. These included such applications as:

- intrusion detection systems,
- checklists for evaluating various control conditions,
- training,
- database query,
- monitoring and review activity and
- general auditing assistance.

The applications ranged in complexity from relatively simple to quite complex in both design and implementation.

MOTIVATION FOR ES

In many cases, the primary motivation for becoming involved in Expert Systems design and development activity was the need for technological assistance to deal with large volumes of transactions that either were very difficult to review and audit or were not feasible to adequately review due to personnel or budgetary restrictions. Increased auditor efficiency and productivity were cited as other dominant reasons for becoming involved with Expert Systems.

PROJECT DESIGN AND DEVELOPMENT

In almost all cases, the ES projects were conceived in the internal audit department of the firms. In some cases, the actual development was done by internal audit staff. In some cases this development did not utilize resources from other systems development departments or groups in the firm such as MIS. In other cases the development was accomplished by working with either systems groups within the firm or with outside consulting firms. For some of the firms interviewed, the availability of personal computers and/or workstations and off-the-shelf software products such as expert systems shells, facilitated this design and development activity. In several cases, the most important characteristic of the design and development activity appeared to be the domain expertise; that is, the familiarity of internal auditors with internal audit problems was more important to successful design than having professional AI/ES engineers involved in the projects.

PROCESSING PLATFORM

Several firms developed the ES for use in a mainframe environment. The intrusion detection and monitoring systems typically are implemented in mainframe environments. These systems must be integrated with the existing information systems and thus are somewhat complex in nature. Other systems are utilized in a personal computer and/or workstation environment. These systems are not integrated and are used by auditors for various review and diagnostic tasks. Some firms are extracting data from the mainframes and reviewing the data with PC based expert systems tools.

OTHER BENEFITS

In addition to the benefits suggested by the motivation section above, several firms suggested other benefits from embracing the ES technology. These included marketing benefits, that is, positive publicity about ES development activities that enhance the image of the internal audit function within the firm and the firm in general in the marketplace. Other benefits included the possibility of marketing the expert system to other firms with similar problems. In some cases the internal audit function was used as a "test area" to demonstrate feasibility of ES activity for other departments/groups within the firm.

Details of the interviews with each firm now follow. The first firm is identified by name, TRW, for several reasons: (1) this was the first interview and was used to develop and test the survey questionnaire. (2) TRW is in close proximity to the researchers and the chairman of the research committee for this project was at the firm. These factors enabled an "iterative" type interview where several discussions could and did take place. (3) Many of the issues identified with TRW are applicable to the other firms interviewed but are not restated in those interview descriptions to avoid redundancy in this report. (4) The systems described for TRW have received a good deal of publicity in various business publications and the firm has no objections to further being identified. Other firms in the study are only described in general industry terms.

INTERVIEW WITH TRW

The first interview was with TRW. Much of the information in that discussion set the stage for the remaining interviews.

Expert System Application: *Discovery*

One of the first and among the best known of the internal audit expert systems is TRW's "Discovery." Since this system is written up in more detail elsewhere, e.g., Tener [1988], we will not discuss the nature of the system here.

At the time of this report, TRW was believed to be the only credit information service company that uses software to monitor the use of the credit maintenance and reporting system. Apparently few economic incentives exist to monitor such a system. For example, if a subscribing company's employee performs "extra transactions", then the costs of that extra use are passed back to the subscriber.

KNOWLEDGE ACQUISITION

Initially, gathering knowledge was difficult. Oftentimes the experts did not recognize what knowledge would be appropriate for the system. For example, it was common sense to the expert that the time of the day and the day of the week were important statistics in performing their task but initially the experts did not identify these as key factors for the system being developed. This is due in part because the knowledge required for this process had not been previously structured prior to system development.

New knowledge is continually added to the system. The Expert Systems Manager (ESM) (discussed below) is constantly searching out new information to add to Discovery. For example, one of the approaches to acquiring new knowledge is to periodically monitor various hacker bulletin boards to determine if information is posted on how to break into TRW's computers or if generic information is posted that could be helpful to TRW.

TESTING OF THE SYSTEM

When the system was first developed some "false" problems were found by the system. For example, the system might indicate that there was a problem at bank Y, because it had a record of transactions from that bank on a Sunday. However, certain types of banks have transactions on Sunday. Thus, this knowledge had to be built into the knowledge base. Such anomalies can be used to find knowledge that needs to be added to the system.

SUCCESS OF THE SYSTEM

Discovery is able to analyze large volumes of data of client use to determine if there are any unusual patterns. A human would take hours to analyze what Discovery analyzes in minutes. Discovery analyzes the data and reports anomalies the next day. Human investigators would take 30-60 days to find the problem, often too late to take remedial action.

Discovery is used by the investigator because there is a high probability that if it provides a lead then there is a security problem. The usefulness of the system is dependent on not providing incorrect information to the user. The experts do not want to be in a position of suggesting a problem exists and then having the client find no problem. Instead, the system makes them the "hero" by allowing them to state, with small probability of error, "that it looks like there is a problem."

This also suggests that one of the means of measuring the success of the system is to measure the number of leads suggested by the system that ultimately are identified as frauds.

Expert System Application: *Data Edit*

TRW also uses expert systems in data edit. Subscribers provide TRW with magnetic tape summaries of, e.g., their accounts receivables. Since TRW does not require a standard input from these users, there can be a substantial effort to get the information into a standard format. Expert systems technology was chosen as a means to standardize data input tapes.

The system is integrated into the work flow of the subscriber analysis data edit process and is operational. The initial prototype of the system had approximately 10-20 rules that accounted for about 90% of the data edit problems.

The system now has about 100 rules. Many of the additional 80-90 rules were client specific.

Impact of the System. The process of editing client data had been a labor intensive effort requiring about 50 clerks. With the use of this expert system, the number of clerks has dropped to about 25. At this time, no measures of effectiveness or of job enrichment have been developed.

Expert System Application: *Maintenance of the Credit Database*

Periodically, the credit database requires maintenance. For example, individuals may dispute the status of their account. An account may be reported to TRW as "paid" or "paid charge-off" and TRW will want to make the changes consistent. Thus, the client may indicate to TRW that they want to change a data element from x to y. However, a human expert examining the change might question the change since instead of x it should be z. This suggests that there are certain rules that are used to analyze the data for appropriateness.

ORGANIZATIONAL ISSUES

In each of the above applications, TRW found that the initial and continued success of an expert system is dependent on two unique organizational roles: expert system champion and expert system manager.

Expert System Champion. TRW feels that the initial success of an expert system is based in large measure with having an expert system champion (ESC). The ESC is someone willing to put himself/herself behind the development effort and the selling effort to management and the rest of the organization. The interviewees at TRW felt it was helpful to have an ESC in order to facilitate the development and implementation of the system.

Expert System Manager. With most computer programs when the system is operational and ready to go into production this means that the system will require only minimal amounts of additional programmer intervention. Programmers move on to other projects. Otherwise the system is a "flop." However, unlike other computer programs, many expert systems need constant "care and feeding." The knowledge base must continue to change as the environment changes. New knowledge must be put into the knowledge base as it is discovered. In the case of expert systems such constant attention is not a sign that the program is a "flop." Instead, it is likely to indicate that the problem which the system is designed to solve is dynamic and lacks easily elicited structure.

Because expert systems continue to evolve and change over time, TRW has found need for an expert system manager (ESM) to monitor the development of the system over time. The *ESM* is somewhat analogous to a database manager. Although not necessarily initially a true expert in the area of the application, the *ESM* is now a "near expert" in the domain. The *ESM* has both a reactive and a proactive role in continuing the development of the expert system. The *ESM* can add knowledge that the user would like to be a part of the system. Further, the *ESM* can generate new knowledge for the system. The *ESM* can question the system output.

KNOWLEDGE ACQUISITION

For each of the systems, one of the primary sources of knowledge and tests of the existing knowledge is the anomaly. Typically, this is something that the system cannot explain, and thus, additional knowledge must be added to allow the system to explain the problem. However, not every anomaly should be a part of the database. This is because some anomalies are in conflict with others or with existing knowledge.

The TRW experience also suggests that expert systems can be developed more efficiently and more rapidly if the developer also is an expert in the problem domain. This is consistent with reviews of other studies found in the literature review.

This finding indicates that when putting together the expert system development team the expert needs to be actively involved in the process and the expert really needs to be a "true" expert. Too often, the team consists of available personnel, which may not be expert personnel. Further, since the expert may be active in other projects the development of the current system may receive a subordinated priority from the expert.

BENEFITS FROM EXPERT SYSTEMS

The TRW experience indicates that the benefits from implementing an expert system go beyond the direct benefits of increased output, higher quality and decreased operational personnel. TRW also experienced two additional benefits. First, TRW received extensive publicity on the system, thus, developing goodwill. Second, much of the data developed for one of the expert systems also can be used for marketing purposes.

In particular, the usage data from which the portfolios are established provides marketing information. Determining the purposes for which the client uses the database also establishes those aspects of that database which the client does not exploit. Those findings can be used to market additional use of the database.

DANGERS OF THE USE OF EXPERT SYSTEMS

There are a number of dangers with the integration of expert systems into an organization. First, if there is an expert system then there is a tendency for the human to not examine the issues with the same critical eye that would be used if the system was not there. This can lead to a decrease in the quality of results produced by the man-machine combination.

Second, after the system has been in place for a period of time a tendency exists to forget the system is there. This can prove to be a disaster if the process being examined changes, and the system does not. Similarly, if the system provides "default" values rather than requesting them from the user the presence of the system may be disguised and possible difficulties or inconsistencies in the input data may not be observed.

CONTROLS AND AUDITING EXPERT SYSTEMS

The existence of expert users of the expert system and an *ESM* provide a control over the knowledge in the knowledge base. Since the *ESM* at TRW is a near expert, the *ESM* provides an audit check over the information that the expert user requests which the *ESM* put into the system. Further, since the user is an expert, there is a check on the information placed in the system by the *ESM*.

Thus far, auditing of the expert systems at TRW has not proved difficult (from a perspective of understanding the process on which the system is based) because for each of the applications the audit group will audit, there is an expert in the audit group staff in that area.

However, there is concern for the time when that is not the case. Then such issues as "How much do you depend on a user?" become of prime concern.

Another issue of concern at TRW is at what time do auditors get involved in the expert system design and development process. For virtually all accounting systems an auditor is involved in the design and development process at some point relatively early on, so that the appropriate controls can be built into the system.

Looking toward the future, the primary needs of the project team are the development of generic audit plans and audit tools for the audit of expert systems.

INTERVIEW WITH A DEPARTMENT STORE CHAIN

The director of internal audit of a large department store chain also was interviewed. He indicated that firm did not use expert systems technology. However, some of the discussion in that interview led to an investigation of some potential applications of expert systems in internal auditing in the retail industry. The company did not use expert systems technology because management is uncomfortable with computer-based systems and accounting information systems.

NEED FOR EXPERT SYSTEMS AT DEPARTMENT STORES

Clearly expert systems could be used in department stores in a manner similar to TRW to detect fraud. For example, trends in inventory or other financial indicators could be used to find potential fraud; also credit application review and charge card abuse can also benefit from applying ES technology.

Currently, it may be difficult for accountants to find fraud using financial information because the department stores are so large that fraudulent transactions may easily slip through the cracks. Unfortunately, in most larger department stores it would be impossible for humans to directly analyze financial information for all available cost centers. However, an expert system could easily examine all the cost centers and provide the human investigator with those suspected cases that warrant further investigation. This suggests that instead of having expert systems examine the total aggregated financial statements, attention be focused at lower levels of aggregation. This may be at the lowest responsibility center level.

There could be other applications. For example, assume that the information system produces information by store on a daily basis. Currently humans are responsible for shifting inventory from store to store to ensure that it is sold. An expert system could be responsible for this activity, since there may be too many decisions required to be made in too short a period of time. Further, such a system could ensure that such decisions have a certain consistency.

SPECIFIC TECHNIQUES

Some techniques can be embedded in expert systems and used to analyze, e.g., databases for the existence of fraud. To a certain extent the approach used to detect fraud would be a function of the particular cycle or the particular firm or both. For example, the vendor database could be analyzed using a number of techniques including:

- Ascertain if any of the vendors have different names but the same address.

- Ascertain if any of the vendors have the same names but different addresses.

- Ascertain if any of the vendor names or addresses are similar to purchasing employee names or addresses.

- Ascertain if the person who received the goods is different than the person who ordered the goods. For example, if goods were ordered and received by the same person then there is an opportunity for fraud.

- Ascertain if the purchasing behavior of the employee changes (ala TRW). This could include items purchased, number of orders per day, dollar volume of purchases, etc.

- Ascertain if the purchasing behavior from particular vendors has changed (ala TRW). This could include items purchased, number of orders, dollar volume of purchases, time between goods ordered and received, etc.

In the areas of accounts receivables a similar list can be developed. For example,

- As part of the system of accounts receivable, capture the name of the person putting through the credit. Then compare the name and address of that person to the person or firm for whom the payment has been credited.

- Ascertain if the payment behavior of the account receivable has changed, e.g., date of payment, full or partial payment, amount of payment, etc.

- Ascertain if the person performing the accounting work on the account is the normal person for that account, is the time of day unusual, etc.

INTERVIEW WITH A FORTUNE 100 MANUFACTURING FIRM

This company has done substantial in-house promotion of the use of artificial intelligence, including offering courses to employees on the use of expert systems. Through these promotional efforts and information obtained from external sources, the internal audit organization of this company recognized the potential for using expert systems in support of audit activities and has dedicated resources to exploring this potential.

Application: *Automated Audit Checklist*

The initial application undertaken by this firm is an automated checklist designed to assist financial and EDP auditors in evaluating data processing controls for application systems supporting financial and business functions subject to audit review. The application is designed to facilitate workpaper preparation and to supplement auditor knowledge and judgment by:

1. Providing the auditor with the right set of questions,

2. Offering background information regarding the importance of specific controls,

3. Assisting the auditor in identifying potential problem areas which warrant attention/follow-up,

4. Suggesting compliance tests to evaluate the effectiveness of the controls in place.

Since many internal auditors do not fully understand the control requirements for complex computer-based systems, this application is being developed to promote an integrated audit approach that encompasses the evaluation of controls both within and outside the computer. The system is designed for use in a PC environment.

INTERVIEW WITH A FORTUNE 100 COMPUTER FIRM

An approach aimed at the entire audit process is being designed and implemented by the internal auditors of a Fortune 100 computer firm. The focus of this company is on the development of computer assisted auditing tools (CAAT). Their approach is based on first accessing database elements and then choosing appropriate database elements for audit. The system design also includes adding auditing intelligence to the system to further assist the auditor in the investigation of the data. The system breaks the financial information of a firm into:

1. Accounts Payable

2. Payroll

3. Purchasing

4. Inventory

5. Billing

6. General Ledger

The system takes an accounting database and maps that database into a CAAT database. Once in a CAAT database, the user can query the database and perform statistical sampling of the database. The system also allows the auditor to develop ad hoc reports from the CAAT database.

The system allows the user to extract data elements from the database to audit the financial information. Those elements can be of an ad hoc nature. However, the system also is designed to provide audit programs with each of the individual processes. Once the set of audit tasks is selected the system will choose the data elements necessary to perform those tasks.

The firm initially has been concerned with building a system to support auditor decision making. Future work on the system will be aimed at building auditor expertise into the investigation of each of the processes. To facilitate use, the system is designed to be menu driven.

Because of the firm's size, the system is based in a mainframe environment. As was noted in the interview, the number of transactions are in the "billions." As a result, current personal computers would be an inappropriate environment.

Further, the system is designed for a multinational environment that will allow the user in the US to perform an audit of a company or branch in almost any other country. Such an approach limits the amount of travel necessary to audit information from other countries.

The internal financing for the system is based on the firm's turning the system into a viable product. It is anticipated to be sold to other companies.

INTERVIEW WITH A LARGE WEST COAST BANK

Large banks face an environment which involves a large volume of transactions that involve the most liquid of assets: cash. Further, decisions about those transactions must be made in a real time manner. In addition, to meet increasing amounts of competition, bank internal audit departments are continually asked to cut back on their personnel. Thus, the banks are continually looking for new tools, such as expert systems to facilitate their audits.

INTER-BANK CLEARING ACCOUNT

One particular concern of internal audit is auditing inter-bank transactions, i.e., the clearing account. This is true for a number of reasons. First, there are a "huge" number of transactions to examine. In fact, there are so many transactions that it is impossible for humans to examine all the transactions. Second, because of the nature of the task, the bank has difficulty keeping experienced personnel on the task of reconciling this account.

Internal Auditing for this bank has developed an expert system for investigating unusual and fraudulent transactions that appear in a branch clearing account, i.e., Inter-Branch transactions. The system is a rule-based system that employs rules that account for the following concerns, among others.

- "Offset should not come from the same branch as the originator of the transaction"

- "Break-down entries that add up"

- "Are there an extraordinary amount of entries from a given branch?"

- "Do transactions roll forward?"

PORTABILITY OF APPLICATIONS TO OTHER BANKS

Although this and other banks have developed expert systems, there may be only limited portability of the applications from bank to bank. A number of factors limit this portability. First, different banks have different forms, requiring different information. Second, different banks have different rules of processing.

On the other hand, other reasons exist for substantial portability between different banks. For example, regulatory requirements are similar between different banks. Further, because of the similarity of business from bank to bank, the needs of banks are likely to be the same.

INTERVIEW WITH A STOCK BROKERAGE FIRM

One of the larger stock brokerage firms is developing an expert system to assist in the internal audit of branch offices. The system is being developed in LISP (a specialized AI programming language) for a personal computer environment with the assistance of the consulting department of a large international accounting firm.

Currently, the audit of branch offices is a labor intensive activity. Unfortunately, the internal audit department is unable to obtain enough quality staff to meet its needs. Thus, it is desirable to increase the productivity of the existing staff. In addition, much of the audit staff for that activity is junior staff. Thus, it is desirable to train existing staff and ensure consistency of judgment of the junior staff.

To accomplish these goals a system was designed to assist the auditor in planning and conducting audits using mainframe data. The system extracts data and uses a personal computer to investigate the data.

The system emphasizes the examination of trends across individual branches. The system provides automated workpapers in conjunction with an on-line intelligent questionnaire. In particular, the system allows sample selection, work paper generation, sample testing, policy document retrieval and auditor comments.

INTERVIEW WITH A LARGE INTERNATIONAL ACCOUNTING FIRM ABOUT A CLIENT'S BROKERAGE SYSTEM

In brokerage firms, branch managers are responsible for monitoring broker activity. Typically, this requires a review of customer statements and the transactions on those statements. Unfortunately, because of the volume of transactions it is very difficult for a manager to do an effective analysis. Accordingly, it is desirable to have the computer perform this task, if possible.

One large international accounting firm in conjunction with a brokerage firm is developing a system to assist branch managers in this task. The system includes many of the rules that managers would use in the investigation of broker activity. Using these rules and profiles (to characterize brokers, customers and securities), the system

- Reviews all customer statements

- Suggests actions and resolutions

- Shows detailed explanation of issues

- Allows for entry of comments during the review

- Keeps track of which brokers and issues have been reviewed and what is left to do.

The system increases branch manager productivity by delegating much of the broker review to the system. Further, because the system increases the scope and detail of analysis, the system improves the management of the brokers.

INTERVIEW WITH A LARGE INSURANCE COMPANY

The internal audit department of this firm has two primary objectives associated with employing expert systems. It is interested in improving both the department's efficiency and effectiveness by using expert systems. The firm also is concerned about future auditing of such systems. As a result, they have built their own system in order to anticipate some of the difficulties and to obtain experiences in expert systems.

Generally, the firm has found that managers have had difficulties coming up with audit concerns. As a result, a system was built to suggest those concerns.

The system is a control analysis application. It has an expert system designed to assist the auditor in addressing the issues in control analysis. However, it is anticipated that eventually, the system will become the property of the operations department.

It is not designed for a specific application, such as cash receipts or disbursements. The system finds out what the managers are doing in their departments, what exposures there are, what must go right, what their concerns are and what controls are used to meet the needs of those concerns.

The next phase of the project is to have the system suggest controls for the corresponding audit concerns. The system was developed using an expert system shell (VP Expert). The system employs a dBase interface to obtain data about the client department.

INTERVIEW WITH A LARGE EAST COAST BANK (A)

The scenario that generated the bank's internal audit department's interest in artificial intelligence and expert systems is "typical." First, turnover in the internal audit department is at about 33% per year, with the most at entry levels. Thus, a vehicle for managing and educating new employees is desired. Second, the bank continues to grow, yet wishes to control the growth of the internal audit department. The department needs to improve efficiency and contain costs. Third, the internal audit department wishes to improve the quality of its audits, while maintaining effectiveness. Fourth, the internal audit department sees the future use of such expert systems growing. As a result, they are concerned about getting some experience in auditing these systems. Fifth, the use of expert systems in a PC environment is consistent with the trend to developing end-user computing tools.

The internal audit department took an active role in examining possible expert systems' applications. A period of about three months was spent doing applications selection. Then project financing was obtained via an internal R&D grant from the bank to the internal audit department.

The application that the bank chose was "Foreign Exchange." The application was regarded as a high growth area, with volume more than doubling in a single year. In addition, the substantial amount of data generated in this application made it a difficult area to audit.

Prior to system development a human auditor could only examine a single day of transactions because of budgetary and time limitations. Such an approach ignores the potential relationships between activity on different days that could be discovered. Thus, foreign exchange was an area that could benefit from an improvement in the audit technology that would facilitate multiple day examinations.

The system examines the trades for "unusual" trades. Such trades are identified using trading and trader knowledge. Portfolios of traders can be developed using information such as time of day, clients, amount of trade and frequency of trade. Information about trades may include trading partners, amount of trade, rates and so on.

Like other expert systems, it is a highly focused system. The scope of the system is limited to sterling and dollar trades. Now that the system is in place, rather than a single day's trades, trades over 30-day increments are now examined. The system design takes into account a number of anomaly variables including: Day of the Week, Fed Actions and Revaluation.

Because of the interest in end user computing, the system was developed on a PC using the expert system shell "First Class." The system has approximately 65-70 rules. However, another 30-35 rules based on the effect of the "time of day" are to be added to the system. The system is an off-line system. An IBM System 38 creates an ASCII file. That file is then examined by the system.

The system also has facilitated the interaction of the internal audit department with the trading department. Until the development of this system, few management tools were available to determine when a trader was doing well and when a trader was not doing well. This system provided such a tool to that department head. In addition, it provided credibility to the internal audit department, so that now the internal auditors have greater accessibility to the head trader.

INTERVIEW WITH A LARGE EAST COAST BANK (B)

The internal audit department of the bank has developed a system to assist in the investigation of the controls for systems development. The system is a smart internal control analyzer, to determine if the controls are adequate. The system is used on every systems review. The system was developed on an IBM AT using GURU, an expert systems shell, and was funded with departmental monies.

One of the concerns in the development of the system was that the system primarily guide and assist the auditor. This is in contrast to other systems that do so much that they may make the auditor stop "thinking." The system was not developed to supplant the person. Instead, the system was designed to help eliminate some of the "grunt" work that comes with audits.

The internal auditors at this bank indicate that it could be too expensive to have each internal audit department develop each possible expert system application. During the interview, they also suggested that many internal auditing tasks were similar from firm to firm. As a result, they suggest that it may be beneficial to have firms that develop a specific package sell those packages to other firms.

In addition, to the extent feasible, they indicate that some of these same expert system packages could be adapted and utilized in operations. Providing operations with expert support and information about the controls and security of those operational departments, could in the long run, increase the security and controls of the particular departments.

INTERVIEW WITH A LARGE AEROSPACE FIRM

A large aerospace firm has many AI projects ongoing in the organization but none in internal audit. The internal auditors interviewed had some difficulty in differentiating between conventional procedural programs such as embedded test routines and expert systems technologies. This interview suggested several issues: one is definitional—what is an expert system? Another issue relates to the transition between conventional programs and expert systems programs. The definitional issue suggested in this interview is that for many systems in internal auditing, there may not be a requirement for high levels of expertise. Rather expert systems technology, such as the separation of data (knowledge) from control or flow of the computer program may be more effective in software development where the environment changes frequently since this kind of system can be updated more easily by simply changing the knowledge portion of the program and not the control or flow. Another issue raised in the interview is how does a firm with limited personnel and budgets, find the impetus to dramatically switch from conventional programs to expert systems even though the benefits can be demonstrated. These issues are not unique as demonstrated in the survey portion of the report.

INTERVIEW SUMMARY

The most common type of expert system encountered in the interview process was characterized as an "intrusion detection" system, also known as a "continuous audit" system or a "fraud detection" system. These systems employ "profiles" of expected behavior. Those profiles are then compared to actual behavior to determine when unusual behavior is encountered. Such unusual behavior is taken as a signal of illegal or inappropriate behavior.

Another common application of expert systems is the checklist or smart checklist. These applications include long lists of activities that could be overlooked without such a system. In addition, these systems allow smart processing of activities. When one activity leads to another activity, the system informs the user. Similarly, when an activity is not required, the system knows what other activities are not required.

Often these two types of applications are dependent on customizing the knowledge to the specific organization and often to specific users. Thus, in many cases they do not offer the ability to port the application to other users and thus without substantial change. Although the sample of firms interviewed was primarily firms that have developed applications, there was considerable bias in favor of the use of such systems. Further, there was substantial variety in the actual applications chosen. The systems ranged from specific checklists to extensive applications that include almost all accounting functions.

Chapter 5

THE MULTIPLE ROLES OF INTERNAL AUDITORS IN THE USE OF EXPERT SYSTEMS:*
A Survey of Internal Auditor Managers

Introduction

Expert systems (ES) constitute an important area of application of artificial intelligence (AI). New advanced information technologies such as ES are being planned, developed and implemented in a variety of business, government and other entities. Although most research has examined the use of ES/AI in auditing for Certified Public Accountants (CPAs) (e.g., Brown [1991]), internal auditors also use ES/AI (e.g., Brown et al. [1991]).

PURPOSE OF THIS CHAPTER

Internal auditors are involved in at least five general roles related to ES/AI: (1) auditors; (2) consumers; (3) developers; (4) managers; and (5) consultants to management. The purpose of this chapter is to explore the impact of ES/AI on each of those five roles. In particular, the purpose of this chapter is to provide descriptive evidence indicating the extent to which internal auditors are involved in all five of

---

*An earlier version of this chapter was presented at the 2nd Annual Workshop on Expert Systems in Accounting, Auditing and Tax, August, 1993.

those roles, with respect to ES/AI. In addition, this chapter is designed to provide some understanding as to the nature of each of these roles and the concerns generated with the impact of a new technology, expert systems, on those roles.

OUTLINE OF THIS CHAPTER

This chapter proceeds as follows. The next section provides background information, including the use of expert systems in internal auditing and the importance of organizational roles in the introduction of new technologies into firms. The following discusses the research questions and contributions. The next section summarizes the methodology. The subsequent two sections investigate the findings. The final section provides a brief summary.

Background

This section provides some brief background information. In particular, it discusses the five roles of internal auditors that are of particular interest and summarizes some issues of concern in the analysis of organizational roles and new technologies of ES/AI.

ES/AI IN INTERNAL AUDITING

There has been limited research on the impact of the use of ES/AI in internal auditing. Virtually all that research has aimed at the analysis of systems that can be or are used in internal auditing (e.g., Brown and Phillips [1991]). For example, Tenor [1988], Halper et al. [1988] and Lecot [1988] discuss the use of intrusion-detection systems to perform tasks such as continuous on-line auditing. TIARA (Inference Corporation) is a system that was designed to assist in the assessment of audit risk. Sen and Wallace [1992] discuss a system designed to assist with the internal audit of banks. Thus, the primary focus of the research on internal auditing and ES/AI has been in the area of specific systems and not on the impact of ES/AI on internal auditors or the roles of internal auditors in organizations.

INTERNAL AUDITOR ROLES

The job of the internal auditor is broad-based, encompassing at least five different roles, in the case of introducing, developing and using expert systems. First, the internal auditor is a consumer of ES/AI technology. Internal auditors use expert systems for a number of different tasks. Second, the internal auditor is a management consultant on ES/AI technology. If the internal auditor is knowledgeable, then he/she can advise management about the use of ES/AI, and the policies and procedures that are necessary to implement ES/AI in a corporate environment. Third, the internal auditor is a developer of ES/AI. Internal auditors have generated a number of applications of AI/ES technology. Fourth, internal auditors function as managers of the use and development of AI/ES technology. As a result, they must understand the strengths and limitations of the technology. Fifth, the internal auditor must audit ES/AI applications. As a result, the internal auditor needs to understand what processes are necessary to provide that activity.

ROLES AND NEW TECHNOLOGIES

Perhaps the most extensive analysis of the impact and use of roles in organizations is Kahn et al. [1964]. They suggest that organizations have roles that demand innovative solutions to nonroutine problems and other roles for those problems that require more routine solutions. Thus, roles play a critical part in the organizational use of new technologies.

Kahn et al. [1964] suggest that innovative roles represent "patterned organizational deviance." They view these innovative roles as a response by organizations to attempt to build into themselves the ability to change.

Each of the five internal auditor roles mentioned above requires innovation in the face of new technologies. As consumers, internal auditors must determine which applications are appropriate for the use of the technology in internal auditing. As consultants, they must understand the technology and its role in the organization. As developers, they must understand the actual use of the new technologies. As managers, they must determine the strengths and weaknesses of the uses of the technologies. Finally, as auditors, they must determine new approaches to audit the new technologies. As a result, the approach taken in this chapter is to explore some aspects of each of these innovator roles required of internal auditors.

Research Questions and Contributions

This research is issue-oriented and is not directly concerned with detailed technical issues or programming languages. The major goal of this chapter is to address the multiple ES/AI issues that confront internal auditors in their roles as auditors, consumers, consultants, managers and developers of ES/AI technology. Accordingly, five major research questions were identified:

1. To what extent are internal auditors using ES/AI technology and what types of applications are being used or planned (the consumer role)?

2. What consulting roles are internal auditors playing in the development of ES/AI technology (the consultant role)?

3. To what extent are internal auditors developing expert systems and what environments are they using (the developer role)?

4. What obstacles and benefits are generated from the use of ES/AI technology (the management role)?

5. What new audit and security issues are generated for internal auditors from ES/AI (the auditor role)?

The contribution of the research is to provide insight into the use of ES/AI in particular, and a new technology, in general, by internal auditors. In addition, the research identifies critical issues of concern to internal auditors and management. This study also provides insights into the use of artificial intelligence in an important domain in corporations, internal auditing.

BACKGROUND INFORMATION

The findings for each question are discussed separately.

Question 1: Please indicate the approximate annual sales for your firm.
The response to the question indicated that the very largest US firms participated with sales figures in the billions of dollars category as well as some smaller firms with sales in the low six figure area. For some entities, annual sales are not appropriate and those entities indicated so accordingly. The main benefit of this question was to determine that a good cross section of firms was represented, both small and large.

Question 2: Please indicate the type of industry in which you would classify your firm, for example, financial services, high technology, aerospace, etc.
Table 5-1 presents a summary of the number of firms responding to the questionnaire by industry. Thirty industries were identified by the respondents and these are listed in Table 5-1 as 22 major indus-

Table 5-1

RESPONDENTS BY INDUSTRY AND DEGREE OF
FAMILIARITY WITH EXPERT SYSTEMS

Industry	Not Familiar	Familiar	Total
Financial Services	118	125	243
Insurance	40	32	72
Government	32	61	93
Utility	29	32	61
Education	18	37	55
Conglomerate	4	1	5
Manufacturing	51	59	110
Telecommunications	8	14	22
Hi-Tech	12	14	26
Non Profit	2	0	2
Retail	10	25	35
Wholesale	2	10	12
Oil & Gas	14	10	24
Construction	4	10	14
Health	12	29	41
Food	7	5	12
Transportation	3	9	12
Aerospace	5	4	9
Agriculture	2	3	5
Publishing	2	9	11
Entertainment	2	3	5
Miscellaneous	26	14	40
Total	403	506	909

tries, with 8 industries being included in the Miscellaneous category. Examples of firms in the miscellaneous category include automotive maintenance and repair, forest products, consulting services, building maintenance and so on. Table 5-1 also shows the total number of respondents represented in each industry category.

Question 4: Please indicate the degree of general familiarity you (the internal auditor) have with artificial intelligence and/or expert systems.

Respondents were asked to indicate no, low, moderate or high familiarity. 55.68% of the respondents had no familiarity with ES/AI. 22.82% had low familiarity, 20.09% moderate familiarity and 1.42% high familiarity. Thus, at least 45.23% of the respondents had at least some familiarity with ES/AI technologies.

The financial services industry had the greatest number of firms familiar with ES/AI(118), followed by manufacturing(51), insurance(40), government(32), and utilities(29). These numbers are somewhat misleading since the financial services industry also had the largest number of firms not familiar with ES/AI, followed by insurance, manufacturing, government and utilities. On a percentage basis, 48.56% of the financial services industry respondents were familiar with ES/AI contrasted to 51.44% of the respondents who were not familiar with ES/AI. Those respondents not familiar with ES/AI were asked to return the questionnaires after responding to this question. The remaining respondents were familiar with ES/AI and completed the remaineder of the questionnaire. The percentages given in the subsequent paragraphs of this section of the report are percentages of those respondents familiar with ES/AI.

CONSUMER ROLE

Question 5: To what extent are you employing expert systems, artificial intelligence technologies, as part of the internal audit function?
This is a question regarding a consumer's role. 68.51 % of the respondents replied none, 24.18% replied low, 6.30 replied moderate, and 1.01% replied high. Thus, approximately one-third of the internal audit functions within respondent firms were, to some extent, were employing ES/AI technologies.

Question 8: Please indicate the areas below which you believe have potential for the application of artificial intelligence/expert systems technologies in support of internal auditing in your firm.
Ordered by magnitude of percentages the results are: Smart Questionnaires (18.71%), Audit Risk Assessment (17.82%), embedded audit routines (14.76%), audit planning (12.75%), analytical review assessment (11.09%), financial fraud detection (9.74%), decision aids (8.46%), and personnel scheduling (6.67%). In addition, this question asked for any applications that the respondents wished to indicate that were not included in the above list. As shown in Table 5-2, a large number of potential applications areas were indicated ranging from

Table 5-2

ADDITIONAL POTENTIAL ES/AI APPLICATIONS FOR
INTERNAL AUDITING

Aid of performance of audit in complex areas

Audit Program Development

Audit Reporting

Budget Projections/Actual

Canned Audit program e.g., expert auditor from MIS training

Contracts

Credit Profile Analysis

Detection of Problem Areas: Production, Customer Service, etc.

Direct Observation of Risk Kinetics

Disaster Recovery Planning

EDP Application Controls Reviews

EDP Auditing

EDP Systems Development

Evaluating Sample Results

Evaluation & Documentation

Exception Database Monitoring

Financial Analysis

Financial Product Development

Flagging/Warning Key Indicators

Flowcharting, Samples

Highly Technical Audits

Information Access and Security

Internal Control Evaluation

Inventories

Large Audit Staff Management

Loan Classification Review

Maintenance Scheduling

Manual Calculates Automation

Microcomputer Auditing

Modeling

On-line Computer Systems

Operating System Auditing

Operation System Software Implementation

Policies/Procedures

Product Mix

Production Scheduling

Real-time Security Controls

Review of On-Line (mainframe) Accounting and Payroll Data

Risk exposure analysis

Sampling/Testing Accounts

Specific Audits (e.g., CICS)

Spread Sheets

Statistical Sampling Design

System diagnostics and software "help" files on the best user action to be taken to make current applications much more user friendly

System error messages and most appropriate order to do corrective actions

Technical MIS Audits

Training

Union Contract Exceptions

Word Processing

Working Papers

disaster recovery planning, to data integrity analysis to statistical sampling and so on.

Question 9a: How many ES/AI applications are you using?

38 firms were using one ES/AI system, 29 firms were using two systems, 8 firms were using three systems, 4 firms were using four systems and 1 to 2 firms each were using somewhere between five and 40 ES/AI systems. 87 firms responding were utilizing ES/AI applications.

CONSULTANT ROLE

Question 6: To what extent is the internal audit function involved in providing input for management decisions regarding acquisition, development and usage of artificial intelligence / expert systems in your firm?

It was found that 53.20% are not providing input, 33.25% are providing low input, 11.82% are providing moderate input and 1.72% are providing high input. Thus, about 45% were providing some input to management related to ES/AI technologies.

Question 7: To what extent is the internal audit function developing policies, procedures and plans for dealing with issues related to artificial intelligence / expert systems technologies in the firm?

57.64% were not currently developing plans, policies and procedures, 29.80% indicated a low level of development, 11.58% indicated a moderate level of development and .99% indicated a high level of development of plans, policies and procedures. Thus, about 42% of the respondents appeared to be developing some plans, policies and procedures related to the employment of ES/AI technologies within the firm.

DEVELOPER ROLE

Question 9b: How many ES/AI applications are you developing?

It was found that 29 firms were developing one application, 12 firms were developing two applications, 4 firms were developing 3 applications and from 1 to 2 firms each were developing from four to eight applications. A total of 50 firms were in the development phase of ES/AI applications.

Question 9c: How many ES/AI applications are you (the internal audit department) planning?

98 firms were planning future applications ranging from one to ten for each of the firms responding. 54 were planning one application,

31 were planning two, 10 were planning three, and 3 were planning four or more.

Question 10a: Please indicate the ES/AI hardware development environment you are utilizing.

10.20% were using mainframe computers exclusively, 46.94% are utilizing small computers - mini/micros and 42.86 were using a combination of both micro and mainframe computing environments to develop ES/AI technologies.

Question 10b: Please indicate the ES/AI software development environment you are utilizing.

61.59% of the respondents were using Expert Systems shells, 15.24% were using specialized computer programming languages such as LISP and PROLOG and 23.17% were utilizing other tools and techniques such as writing the ES programs in procedural programming languages such as COBOL or C.

Question 11: If the internal audit function has been involved or is going to be involved in designing, developing and implementing expert systems technologies, how did (do) you plan to acquire the expertise necessary to proceed?

61.24% of the respondents indicated that they plan to train their existing staff. 26.33% plan to utilize outside consultants while 6.51% plan to hire AI/ES experts. The remaining 5.92% plan to enter into jointly funded projects with either outside or inside consultants.

MANAGER ROLE

Question 9d: How many ES/AI application are you not utilizing?

This question is focused on determining how many ES/AI applications which have been developed, are not currently being used for whatever reason. 122 firms responded that they had from 1 to 4 applications that had been developed but were not being utilized. Many of these developed applications may have been prototypes that allowed internal audit staffs to gain exposure to ES/AI technologies.

Question 15a: What benefits do you currently experience or anticipate experiencing from use of ES/AI technologies in the internal audit function of your firm?

The percentages of respondents ordered according to magnitude were as follows: more efficient utilization of existing audit expertise (65.90%), more confident decision making (58.88%), enhanced ability to constantly monitor complex situations (53.69%), more timely decision making(49.23%), more rapid development of novice employees through interaction with AI/ES technology (45.43%), cost savings (38.68%), enhanced image as technology leader (34.86%), reduced labor costs (28.57%), migrating applications from internal auditing to operations (19.34%). Since respondents could indicate multiple benefits, the percentages above do not sum to 100%.

Question 15b: What obstacles do you currently experience or anticipate experiencing from use of ES/AI technologies in the internal audit function of your firm?

The percentages of respondents ordered according to magnitude were as follows: lack of trained personnel (68.88%), identifying and extracting human expertise for developing expert systems (55.22%), lack of budget resources (50.76%), difficult to define appropriate areas for which to apply the AI/ES technologies (45.43%), long development cycles (41.98%), selling management on appropriateness of AI/ES for internal audit (39.95%), open-ended nature of some AI/ES projects (29.26%), and inadequate computer resources (20.15%).

AUDITOR ROLE

Question 16 required that the respondent provide open-ended responses to the following question:

Question 16: To what extent do you anticipate new problems in auditing and securing expert systems. Please explain your response.

The responses to question 16 can be grouped under three different topics:

- Logic and Knowledge base Problems

- Identification of an Appropriate Audit Trail

- No New Problems - Extensions of Old Methods

GROUP: LOGIC AND KNOWLEDGE BASE PROBLEMS

The general themes underlying logic problems have to do with issues such as verifying the logic of the system. Since expert systems are often developed using "shells" the decision making logic may not be clearly available or identifiable by auditors. In addition, the issues of whose logic and knowledge is being verified and what basis exists for that logic and/or knowledge are of concern. Even if the logic/knowledge is reasonable, in general, how do auditors determine if it is appropriate for a given application? Other themes include the difficulty in establishing the proper basis for the logic and tracing the logic paths in the ES programs

The logic in expert systems is often dependent on the manner in which knowledge is represented in the expert system. A common form of representation of knowledge is through the use of "if-then" rules. The use of rules presents challenges in the minds of respondents such as: how to provide exhaustive testing of the rules; how to evaluate the interrelationship among the rules; how to insure that proper authorization exists and is utilized in the changing of the rules; and how to ensure that the rules are "correct" and the decision points are functioning properly. Thus, determining the overall "correctness" of the system for a given problem domain is perceived to be a major challenge for auditors. Related to the issues of "correctness" of the system are the issues of "sufficiency" of the system. That is, how can auditors be assured that the system contains the necessary and sufficient considerations for providing advice in a particular application area?

Closely related to the notion of inference in the ES is the factual, procedural and domain knowledge represented in the system. Since internal auditors are more familiar with auditing procedures, policies and standards, auditing of a "knowledge" base will present new challenges. Among the challenges are the setting of standards for knowledge base evaluation. Issues of adequacy of knowledge and relationship of knowledge quality to decision outputs will be crucial for internal audit consideration.

GROUP: ISSUES CONCERNED WITH IDENTIFICATION OF PROPER AUDIT TRAIL

A general theme in this category is the general difficulty in identifying and establishing a proper audit trail for ES.

For example, some respondents expressed concern about the potential lack of documentation standards over updates to the knowledge base which would present concerns with respect to an adequate audit trail. Additional audit trail concerns were expressed due to the complexity of some expert systems which don't facilitate easy identification of audit trails. The potential difficulty in verifying the audit trail components of the expert system were also cited due to inexperience of both developers and auditors of expert systems.

It was suggested that AI/ES technologies are similar to computers in general and more recently PCs. The people using them will resist putting in effective controls at the start and therefore the ability to use, update, review and manage and audit such applications will become very difficult during their early lives.

GROUP: NO NEW PROBLEMS—JUST EXTENSION OF CURRENT TECHNOLOGY/METHODS

This category deals with perceived issues relating to the "new" technology of Expert Systems. Some auditors expressed the view that Expert Systems are just extensions of current technology and that basically no new problems are anticipated. Several respondents felt that the problems with expert systems were not really new but analogous to the migration from batch to real-time systems, that is, going from a paper audit trail to a hidden or nonexistent audit trail. Other respondents used the analogy of moving from auditing around the computer to auditing through the computer as a basis of comparison for "new" problems anticipated in moving to expert systems: that is, no really new problems just a requirement for a change in thinking an understanding the environment plus new techniques.

Although not presenting new problems for auditors per se, some respondents felt that management would have difficulty initially understanding issues such as increased scope of audits encompassing expert systems and the need for review of rules in systems, and assessing the validity of choices of experts who provide expertise for expert systems.

SUMMARY OF ROLES

The results provide an insight into the impact of ES/AI on five roles of internal auditors: consumers, consultants, developers, managers and auditors.

CONSUMERS

Internal auditors are consumers of ES/AI technology. Over 30% responded that they were making some use of ES/AI as part of the internal audit function (Question 5). The respondents indicated a wide range of applications for ES/AI in internal auditing (Question 8). The number of applications varied substantially (Question 9a).

CONSULTANTS

Internal auditors function as consultants to management regarding ES/AI technology. It was found that about 50% of the respondents provided some input to management regarding acquisition, development and usage of ES/AI (Question 6). Further, it was found that slightly over 40% were developing plans, policies and procedures at some level related to the employment of ES/AI (Question 7).

DEVELOPERS

Internal auditors are also involved in the role of developers of AI/ES. A number of firms are developing applications (Question 9b). Further, about 100 firms reported planning the development of an ES/AI system (Question 9c).

The hardware developments vary substantially, but about 90% include mini/micro computers at some level (Question 10a). The software environments also vary, with about 60% using expert system shells, 15% using an AI language and the remainder using other programming languages (Question 10b).

Internal auditors planned to obtain the necessary expertise for designing, developing, and implementing expert systems in a number of different ways including training their existing staff over 60% and hiring consultants (Question 11) over 25% .

MANAGERS

Since internal auditors are consumers and developers of ES/AI technology, there are also managerial concerns. An important issue for managers of ES/AI systems is why systems are not being used (Question 9d). In addition, managers must weigh the benefits and obstacles in determining as to whether or not to use ES/AI technology (Questions 15a and 15b).

AUDITORS

Internal auditors are auditors of ES/AI technology as shown by their concerns raised in the open-ended question (Question 16). The two primary issues concerned the quality of the knowledge base logic and identification of the audit trail. Opinions of the impact on audits varied substantially, from the perspective that there was no difference from that indicating a need to rethink the audit of such systems entirely.

Open-Ended Question

Question 17: Please make any open-ended comments you wish concerning artificial intelligence/expert systems technologies and the issues which internal auditors will face in dealing with these technologies as users, developers, advisers to management and as auditors.

The responses were analyzed by the researchers independently and then compared for their classifications. There were few differences of classification by the researchers. Thus the comments remained grouped according to the following categories.

The responses to question 17 deal with both of the two roles and can be categorized in the following groups.

- Benefits, Positive Prognosis

- Timing, Conservative Views on ES/AI

- Education, Training and Awareness

- Dealing with Appropriate Standards

- Applications Programs, Acquisition of Technology

- ES/AI Development

- Lack of Proper Management and Other Support

- Resources – Time/Cost – Benefits/Management

GROUP: BENEFITS, POSITIVE PROGNOSIS AND RELATED ISSUES

The general theme of this section is that AI/ES will greatly benefit internal auditors and that it is just a matter of time. Many feel that auditors need to "get up to speed" as quickly as possible and become leaders in the implementation of this technology in organizations.

Several respondents suggested that auditing is a fertile area for AI/ES, but new skills and new ways of thinking are required. Auditors must participate in the development of AI/ES systems and be capable of auditing them. This will provide new challenges, perhaps more significant than EDP, for external and internal auditors. However, AI/ES systems are capable of significant payback when properly understood and utilized. Auditors will need to develop better risk models to determine which expert systems to audit. Proliferation will most likely be at such a rate that audit departments will have difficulty in just keeping current with what systems are being developed.

Auditors should derive a great benefit as users of expert systems. They will have access to more information quicker and with less effort. The audit process may not speed up appreciably because the auditor will be doing more analytical work and less detailed information scheduling and gathering.

Respondents noted that AI/ES are technologies in their infancy.

They are having bursts of genius and growing pains. Ten years from now both will be integral parts of all quality accounting and/or audit systems. AI/ES is the new technology. Companies will need to utilize AI/ES or lose their competitive advantage. Auditing has an opportunity to be on the leading edge rather than trailing as in the past. This can only happen if the universities take an active, forward looking approach in their curriculums and organizations such as IIA decide to help find solutions.

Some felt that we are not using AI/ES as effectively as we should. It has good potential for reducing manual work load and provides opportunity to examine a much larger sample than manual procedures. To fall behind users in terms of AI/ES knowledge will be fatal for the auditing profession.

GROUP: TIMING ISSUES AND CONSERVATIVE VIEWS ON ES/AI

Knowing when to embrace the technology and the applicability of the technology to internal auditors appears to be the major theme of this category. Some believe that it will be a fairly long period of time before most internal auditors will be able to utilize or benefit from the technology.

This skepticism seems to be the result of viewing expert systems as an unproven technology or a technology that is too difficult and complex for internal auditors to cope with. Some respondents believe that only the very largest firms will have the resources and ability to utilize ES technologies. Many respondents believe that humans will be adversely affected with the implementation of ES technologies since they may tend to dehumanize decision making and may encourage human users of such systems to stop thinking and questioning assumptions. Other respondents expressed concerns ranging from the notion that AI/ES is just a "fad" to others believing that investment in such technologies would not be cost/beneficial.

GROUP: EDUCATION, TRAINING AND AWARENESS ISSUES

The major concerns expressed in this category have to do with the time and effort required to "keep up" with the technology and the perceived training difficulties and challenges. Fears were expressed relating to the perceived complexity of the ES and the resultant training efforts expected. Internal auditors need to understand the expert systems technology in depth before control issues can be adequately addressed.

A concern was expressed by a number of respondents about the lack of and need for professional organizations to develop and provide training courses and materials for internal auditors in areas of expert systems, particularly from an audit issues point of view. Also of concern to those responding was the need for training strategies within firms which would be forward looking and anticipate where expert systems and other technologies were moving so that proper training could be offered to internal auditors that would give them the "best" available information in assessing and utilizing the expert systems technology.

Auditors as developers, advisers to management and auditors of expert systems will encounter problems if their level of training and expertise does not keep pace with the technology. Companies will have to make a commitment to adequately staff and train auditors to function in an AI/ES environment. This will be the key to properly addressing the AI/ES issue.

Training is important to address now and gain experience so auditors are prepared to audit later. Auditors would benefit from developing an expert system so as to be familiar with issues such as: approach, documentation, testing, cost, reliability and etc.

Some ways must be found for internal auditors to get the necessary training to be able to audit in the AI/ES environment. Budget constraints make this an absorbing task. What is needed is a commitment to staff training. Changing mix of personnel backgrounds from accounting/auditing to engineering/EDP must be addressed.

Concerns were expressed with always being a follower and not a leader or innovator of the technology. There is an acute need to keep abreast of AI/ES technology and scheduled use by firms. Several firms indicated that technology is again ahead of the audit/control community. Auditors continue to stay in a "catch-up" mode. One of the main issues will be continuation of playing "catch-up" with technology. For example, one of the "big 6" external audit firms is implementing a new system geared to the "computer age"—it is great for the age we have recently been in but fails to fit the age we are entering—this will inevitably be the pattern in the future as in the past.

GROUP: ISSUES DEALING WITH APPROPRIATE STANDARDS

With a new technology standards do not exist and the appropriate development of such standards is perceived to be a problem. Since there are no generally agreed upon standards for documentation and terminology for AI/ES, difficulties will exist in setting evaluation standards. In addition, the newness of the technology makes it difficult to evaluate initial projects in AI/ES due to the lack of established, agreed upon standards.

When rule based routines are integrated into large scale transaction systems (e.g., AMEX's credit analyzer), how they drive other traditional elements of the computer support function and how they are installed, certified for wide domain use and monitored will be critical issues which will merge with the broader issues of application migration on to networks and cooperative processing controls between computers of different scale and architecture.

GROUP: APPLICATIONS PROGRAMS AND ACQUISITION OF TECHNOLOGY ISSUES

Major concerns appear to be cost and availability issues. Due to anticipated high costs and lack of readily useful commercial products some respondents appear to be dubious about the utility of ES in their areas. They cite the costs and time for development of in-house tools and want to "wait and see" what commercial vendors can develop for "off-the-shelf" purchase by internal audit groups. Also noted was a general notion of the desirability of off-the-shelf products to facilitate easier utilization of the technology and eliminate some of the perceived high costs of development and training. This acquisition of commercial products also presents potential problems such as vendors' capabilities and willingness to produce reliable logic engines that are controllable and maintain their integrity. Other concerns included the specific nature of AI/ES and the difficulty in finding general purpose application areas for which AI/ES makes sense.

More information is needed from those who have had successful/unsuccessful experiences with AI/ES applications. Also, more information is need about packages available. Since development is costly some auditors will be looking for "developed" systems from the IIA - professional accounting bodies, etc.

Typical audit departments will not invest any time and effort in developing ES. They will more likely purchase ES packages from vendors.

GROUP: DEVELOPMENT ISSUES

The nature of ES is different from conventional systems and a perceived need is how to extend current capabilities and technology to incorporate the "new" technology. Respondents were especially concerned with the proliferation of end-user computing on micros and workstations and the availability of ES shells which facilitate experimentation and ultimately business use without input or involvement from internal auditors. The potential for rapid growth of ES at the end-user level due to proliferation of micros also presents potential audit backlog if internal auditing becomes involved in attempting to establish controls and audit procedures for these systems.

Typically, ES development utilizes prototyping which results in faster development but makes it difficult for internal auditors to be involved in the entire development process. If internal auditors were to assert the need for involvement at the prototyping phase of development, respondents believed that strong resistance would be encountered from the development team since such involvement would slow the development process considerably. In addition, since much ES development does not follow the traditional systems development life cycle (SDLC), reviewing procedures tend to be highly subjective and judgmental.

The use of Expert Systems introduces questions of ownership for system functions as well as ongoing data integrity. Is the system to be maintained by the Expert who designed it, or the developer who built it, or both? As the system matures and "rules" become more complex or just increase, maintenance becomes a significant cost factor. This should be considered during design and system development.

The difficulty in defining appropriate areas for which to apply the AI/ES technologies is also of concern. Extracting relevant data from human experiences (expertise) for maintaining as well as developing the system presents many new challenges.

GROUP: LACK OF PROPER MANAGEMENT AND OTHER SUPPORT

The general theme of this category appears to be fear of being able to "sell" the idea of ES to management and getting management commitment and support. Some respondents suggest that selling any system to management is a problem and AI/ES will be "just that more difficult".

Other respondents noted that internal audit functions are typically understaffed and with new technologies such as AI/ES, finding staff to deal with the new challenges brought about by these technologies will be extremely difficult. Some respondents felt that this technology was beyond the scope of the audit function due to lack of management support and should be addressed by the MIS professionals in the organization. These respondents cited as example cases where EDP audit has not been given much respect by management in traditional systems areas due to a lack of understanding by management. Thus the MIS group has control.

Getting the support of management, in general, for audits has been difficult and to get management support for a new technology will be even more difficult is the view of some respondents. Most respondents agree that getting senior management's support and commitment is critical to internal audit success in dealing with AI/ES issues.

GROUP: RESOURCES—
TIME/COST-BENEFIT/MANAGEMENT

The major problems of lack of staff, lack of budget and lack of time are identified as the major constraints to ES development. In the area of costs several respondents pointed out that given the speed at which AI/ES technology is changing that committing large financial resources for the acquisition of AI hardware/software is not cost effective. Many respondents cited the lack of satisfactory cost/benefit ratios and the difficulty in measuring the benefits realized from AI/ES.

Another major concern was the lack of internal audit staff especially in light of the perceived time requirements for AI/ES related activities. Since the perceived time requirements are great, experienced auditors may be unwilling to invest the time necessary to become proficient in the AI/ES areas.

In large firms where use of ES shells are becoming widespread, some respondents expressed the concern that duplication of effort and resources in multiple areas of the firm which are developing AI/ES would ultimately have a negative impact on the organization by inadequate utilization of resources. This, and the fact that most ES are unique and cannot be utilized outside of the domain for which they were developed makes resource issues of primary concern.

Another key concern is the large development time for ES/AI technology and the general lack of time by internal auditors to accomplish current task loads. Several respondents suggested that budget was not the problem but that lack of personnel who might be involved with AI/ES is a major problem. Since little is known about development activities for ES in other organizations, there is some concern that maintenance and documentation may be very time consuming and costly. Respondents from smaller firms expressed concerns about whether or not they would ever be able to embrace the technology due to resource constraints.

References

Brown, C., "Expert Systems in Public Accounting: Current Practice and Future Directions," *Expert Systems with Applications,* Volume 3, pp. 3-18, 1991.

———, "Expert Systems for Internal Auditing," *Internal Auditor,* August 1991, pp. 23-28.

Halper, F., Snively, J. and Vasarhelyi, M., "The Continuous Audit of On-Line Systems," Unpublished paper presented at the Second International Symposium on Expert Systems in Business, Finance and Accounting (November 1988).

Inference Corporation, "The Internal Audit Risk Assessor (TIARA)," ART Application Note, Inference Corporation, Los Angeles, CA, No date.

Kahn, R., Wolfe, D., Quinn, R., Snoek, J., and Rosenthal, R., *Organizational Stress: Studies in Role Conflict and Ambiguity,* John Wiley & Sons, New York, 1964.

Lecot, K., "Using Expert Systems in Banking: The Case of Fraud Detection and Prevention," *Expert Systems Review,* Volume 1, No. 3, June 1988, pp. 3-22.

O'Leary, D. and Watkins, P., "Review of Expert Systems in Auditing," *Expert Systems Review,* Volume 2, No. 1&2, pp. 3-22, 1989.

Sen, A. and Wallace, W., "An Expert Systems Assistance to Internal Audit Department Evaluation," *Expert Systems with Applications,* Volume 3, pp. 51-66, 1991.

Tenor, W., "Expert Systems for Computer Security," *Expert Systems Review,* Volume 1, Number 2, pp. 3-6, 1988.

INTERNAL AUDITING AND EXPERT SYSTEMS:
Technology Adoption of An Audit Judgment Tool*

Introduction

This chapter is concerned with the analysis of those variables related to the adoption of a technology designed to support accounting and audit judgment. In particular, the purpose of this chapter is to investigate the diffusion of expert systems (ES)/ artificial intelligence (AI) technology, among internal auditors.

ECONOMICS OF DIFFUSION

Researchers in the economics of diffusion generally regard "diffusion" as the "spread" of a technology [Rosegger, 1980]. In some cases "technology transfer" is used to capture the notion of diffusion. From the view of the user, we can talk about adoption of the technology as the ultimate manifestation of that diffusion.

The economics of diffusion has studied such far ranging technologies as strip mining and blast furnaces [Rosegger, 1980]. It is an empirical issue as to whether ES diffuse in a manner similar to such other technologies. The economics of diffusion are discussed further below in the context of ES adoption.

IMPORTANCE OF THE PROBLEM

Determination of the variables that relate to the adoption of audit

---

* An earlier version of this chapter was presented at the American Accounting Association National Meeting, August 1992.

expert systems is a critical issue for a number of reasons. First, under-standing the adoption of ES by internal auditors can be useful as a comparison with the adoption by other users throughout the firm. This would facilitate an understanding of the importance of the functional area.

Second, much of the previous research on technology diffusion and innovation is resident in the economics literature. Thus, one approach to integrating economic-based arguments into expert systems research is to focus on technology diffusion issues. To date there has been little research integrating economics and ES.

Third, if the variables affecting adoption of an internal audit judgment tool are known, then that can facilitate the determination of whether ES are appropriate for a given internal auditor environment. Focusing on those variables that facilitate the introduction of ES allows us to better understand the process of choosing and introducing ES into accounting and auditing.

Fourth, understanding the adoption of ES by internal auditors may facilitate the understanding of the adoption of ES by other accountants and auditors. For example, factors that affect internal auditor adoption of audit judgment technology may be useful in studying public accounting auditors. Many of the issues faced by internal and external auditors are the same and often external auditors use the judgments of internal auditors, although external auditors are in a different corporate environment.

CHAPTER OUTLINE

This chapter proceeds as follows. The next section provides a brief summary of some definitions and of the history of ES use in auditing and internal auditing. The following section investigates the relevant economics research in the area of technology diffusion and summarizes the resulting hypotheses. Then the next section discusses the survey instrument and some measurement issues. The subsequent section summarizes the findings. The final section summarizes the chapter, discusses some contributions and elicits some extensions of the research.

Expert Systems and Internal Auditing

The use of ES in internal auditing was one of the first applications of ES in accounting, auditing or tax. In a sequence of papers, the feasibility of the use of ES in the determination of reasonableness of prices paid for goods in a military purchase system was suggested in

1983 [Dillard et al. 1983]. Flesher and Martin [1987] published the first paper in the general internal auditor literature surveying the use of ES. A recent survey suggests that there were few other applications in the internal auditing literature through 1989 [Brown and Phillips 1991].

INSTITUTIONAL SPONSORED EXPERT SYSTEMS

Although internal auditors may receive information on technologies from a number of different organizations, the Institute of Internal Auditors (IIA) provides information directly to member internal auditors. The IIA has roughly 15,000 members to whom they provide software and publications on different technologies. Prior to this study, the IIA provided at least two sources of information related to ES. The IIA issued software for support of the internal audit process [Boritz 1986]. In addition, a primer on ES was issued by the IIA [Moeller 1987]. Other organizations include the EDP Auditors' Association (EDPAA).

Economic Theory of Diffusion and Innovation

The economic theory of technology diffusion and innovation [e.g., Gold, 1977 and Rosegger 1980] has led to the development of the recognition of a number of factors relating to the ultimate adoption of a technology. Rosegger [1980] summarized those theoretical factors as originating from at least three basic categories: environment, organization and the specific innovation. In this section, that theory is related to each hypothesis i (Hi). The corresponding questions (Qi), used on the survey are listed in Appendix A.

ENVIRONMENT

The environment in which the firm functions can play a critical part in influencing adoption of different technologies. Two variables that have been used to characterize the environment are the type of industry in which the firm is located and the actions of different relevant agencies that directly influence the flows of information regarding innovations to those in a given industry.

Industry. The industry may be helpful in explaining the adoption of ES technology to support internal auditing judgment. For example, certain types of industries, such as insurance, have extensive data processing capabilities. The corresponding staff, equipment and software could facilitate ES adoption, compared to an industry with fewer capabilities. Thus, the hypothesis is that industry impacts the adoption of ES.

Hypothesis 1 (H1) (Q2). The adoption of expert systems technology is related to industry.

Impact of Agencies such as IIA. Adoption of technology requires more than just information about that technology. Carlson [1967] noted that the mere verbal transmission of technical information, which is not used, is not diffusion of technology. Rosegger [1980] found that although transmission or acquisition of information is essential to diffusion, it is not sufficient. Further, in the analysis of one industry [1970], typically "huge" amounts of information in the form of technical papers, exchanges and visits by experts, precede actual increases in diffusion rates.

This finding is critical to organizations and agencies whose aims include the diffusion of information. Although little is known about organizations that support technological diffusion [Gold, 1977] simply providing the opportunity to have information about an innovation does not ensure the adoption. In addition, by ignoring a technology, such agencies may be viewed as providing a negative signal about the technology.

Since large quantities of information have been found as positively related to technology adoption, we would expect that the perceived flow of information from agencies such as the IIA would be positively related to the adoption of the technology.

Hypotheses 2 (H2) (Q14g). The adoption of expert systems is positively related to the perceived information flow received from the IIA.

ORGANIZATIONAL FACTORS

Organization factors can take a number of different forms. The economics of diffusion and innovation point to size variables, opportunity to adopt, pressures to adopt and budget to adopt.

Size. The size of the organization may partially account for the adoption of expert systems technology [Rosegger, 1980]. There are a number of explanations for this, including scale effects, likelihood of having the necessary knowledge to adopt the technology to the specific firm, etc. In internal auditing departments, the size of the department is characterized by the number of internal auditors and the number of internal auditors specializing in EDP applications. Thus, we would expect the adoption of the technology to be positively related to the number of internal auditors or the number of internal EDP auditors or both.

Hypothesis 3 (H3) (Q3a). The adoption of expert systems technology is positively related to the number of internal auditors.

Hypothesis 4 (H4) (Q3b). The adoption of expert systems technology is positively related to the number of internal EDP auditors.

Opportunity and Pressure to Adopt. Kennedy and Thirlwall [1972] differentiate between the opportunity and the pressure to innovate. Opportunity to adopt is a necessary condition for adoption, while pressure to adopt can force the use of a specific technology. The opportunity to adopt expert systems technology in internal auditing could be facilitated if there were general organizational support for ES technology throughout the organization. Such support may include training programs or access to experts in ES (e.g., knowledge engineers). Thus, we would expect a positive relationship between such support and adoption.

Hypotheses 5 (H5) (Q14b). The adoption of expert systems is positively related to the ES support available in the organization.

Pressure to adopt technology can come from within the organization in the form of a corporate strategy or other vehicles. For example, at the time of the study, DuPont made it well known both within the organization and in the press, that corporate plans included the development of a large number of expert systems (2000 systems by 1990, Williamson [1990]). Thus, some of the internal audit departments may have received pressure to adopt ES. As a result, it is assumed that corporate pressure to adopt ES is positively related to the adoption of the technology.

Hypothesis 6 (H6) (Q13). The adoption of expert systems is positively related to firm-wide pressure to adopt the use of expert systems.

Budgetary Pressures. Gold [1964] found that the existence of innovations did not depend so much on the existence of an "innovative" entrepreneur, but instead on the availability of financial and physical resources and on the technical setting of the firm. If there are no resources to spend on the technology, it is unlikely that it will be adopted. Thus, we would expect the existence of budgetary pressures would be negatively related to the adoption of ES—those with no money to invest in the technology are not likely to adopt it.

Hypotheses 7 (H7) (Q14a). The adoption of expert systems technology is negatively related to budgetary pressures

NATURE OF THE INNOVATION

ES and other innovations each have different characteristics that might lead to adoption of the technology. Those characteristics include the economic advantage of adoption, uncertainties associated with use of the innovation, the potential for disruption resulting from adoption of the innovation, and the commitment required for use of ES.

Economic Advantage. Mansfield [1968] indicated that the extent of economic advantage of the innovation over the older methods had a positive impact on the rate of adoption. Thus, if ES can favorably affect the costs of the use of the technology (for example, reduce manpower needs) then the use of expert system could be positively related to economic advantage. Since ES are an "automation of human expertise" we would expect the extent to which there is perceived potential for reduction in manpower to be positively related to adoption of ES in internal auditing.

Hypotheses 8 (H8) (Q14c). The adoption of expert systems is positively related to the perception of the ability of expert systems to reduce manpower needs over manual systems.

Uncertainty. Mansfield [1968] also indicated that two types of uncertainty could influence adoption of technology: the extent of uncertainty associated with the innovation when it first appears and the rate of reduction of the initial uncertainty regarding the innovation's performance.

These two different types of uncertainty translate into two different questions regarding expert systems and internal auditors. First, if internal auditors perceived that there was uncertainty of expert systems to improve the audit process then we would expect there to be a negative impact on adoption. Second, if internal auditors perceived that the uses of expert systems by others were successful, that could reduce the uncertainty of adopting the technology, creating a positive impact on adoption. These are not the same. Improvement of the process does not ultimately result in a successful application, although it might be anticipated that improvement in the process is a necessary condition for a successful application. This results in the following two hypotheses.

Hypothesis 9 (H9) (Q14d). The adoption of ES is positively related to the perception of the certainty of ES to improve the audit process.

Hypothesis 10 (H10) (Q14e). The adoption of ES is positively related to the perception of the success of ES applications.

Disruption Due to Adoption. Simon [1973] indicated that the opportunity costs of failure include not just the cost of the innovation, but the potential consequences of adopting the innovation and then disrupting the entire system or organization. Thus, we would expect that the perceived potential of ES to disrupt operations would be negatively related to the adoption of ES.

Hypothesis 11 (H11) (Q14f). The adoption of ES is negatively related to the perceived ability to disrupt operations beyond the department.

Commitment. Mansfield [1968] found that the extent of commitment required to try out the innovation was an important determinant of the rate of diffusion. An important aspect of commitment is the out-of-pocket costs of such a commitment. At the time of this study, the commitment required to try out ES was quite low. Depending on the awareness of the internal auditors,

inexpensive and easy-to-use ES shells provided the ability to try the technology and develop prototype ES in a personal computer environment. Thus, we would expect adopters to be more aware of the ability to try the technology with minimal commitment.

Hypotheses 12 (H12) (Q14h). The adoption of ES is positively related to the perceived ability to build ES in an inexpensive manner.

Testing the Hypotheses

Only a portion of the survey was devoted to the diffusion of ES technology in internal auditing. Those questions that relate to the diffusion of ES are listed here. They were coded (-1 not true, 0, +1 true). Average response and standard deviation are included in parentheses, as is the outcome of a t-test of the mean, for information purposes. This information is provided for descriptive purposes. Statistical analysis for this and other questions, is discussed further below. All, except Q14c, were significant at the .01 level or better.

Q13   There is firmwide "pressure" to adopt the use of expert systems technologies into departments within your firm, including internal auditing (-.7/.49). (t-test for different than "0" was -28.57)

Q14a Budgetary pressures make it impossible to spend any resources on expert systems in internal auditing (-.22/.69). (t-test for different than "0" was -6.42)

Q14b   There is substantial support available internally for the development of expert systems (-.54/.61). (t-test for different than "0" was -17.83)

Q14c   Expert systems offer advantages in terms of reducing manpower needs over current manual methods (-.02/.61). (t-test for different than "0" was -.655)

Q14d   There is substantial uncertainty that expert systems can improve the audit process (-.15/.7). (t-test for different than "0" was -4.28)

Q14e   Expert Systems developed to date have had very good success (-.12/.54). (t-test for different than "0" was -4.44)

Q14f   Internal audit expert systems have substantial opportunity to disrupt the operations of the firm beyond the scope of the internal audit department (-.58/.6). (t-test for different than "0" was -19.33)

Q14g   There has been substantial flow of information from organizations, such as the IIA and the EDPAA regarding the use of expert systems in accounting and auditing (-.48/.63). (t-test for different than "0" was -15.23)

Q14h   Suitable expert systems can be built for use in internal auditing using inexpensive (e.g., $300) expert system shells (-.067/.63). (t-test for different than "0" was -2.09, while t-test for different than "1" was -33.6)

MEASURING "ADOPTION"

Probably the best measure of "adoption" is whether or not the particular firm adopted ES into the audit process. In order to capture that information, subjects were asked the question 5 "To what extent are you employing ES technology as part of the internal audit function? (0 None, 1 Low, 2 Moderate, 3 High). (.4/.66)." The t-statistic for the mean being different than 0 is 18.3 (.01).

The sample of 406 ("familiar") responses was divided into two samples, based on their answer to that question. Those that answered "none," (68.51%) were treated as a group and those that answered either "low," (24.18%) "moderate,"(6.30%) or "high," (1.01%) were treated as a second group. All the adopters were placed in one group since in each case they had adopted the technology into the audit process. The total populations for each of those two groups were, 278, and 128 respectively.

LOG LINEAR ANALYSIS OF DATA

A log linear model was used to investigate the resulting frequency tables using BMDP [Dixon et al. 1981]. The frequency tables, by percentage in groups, are summarized in the appendix.

The log linear model fits categorical variables by representing cell frequencies as a combination of interactions and main effects. In a two-way analysis of sets A and B, the expected value of a cell (i,j) is represented as $\ln F_{i,j} = t + w_{A_i} + w_{B_j} + w_{AB_{ij}}$, where the w parameters sum to zero over their indices and t is the mean-effect. The log linear process chooses the parameters to solve those equations. The concern in this chapter is with the model AB, the interaction effect of adoption and other variables, in a pairwise analysis, as described in the hypotheses.

The quality of the log linear models (AB) is measured using the Pearson chi-square test. Similarly, the Pearson correlation coefficient, between the observed frequencies and fitted frequencies, is used for determination of direction. The corresponding t-value is used to measure correlation significance.

Survey Findings

These results are summarized in table 6-1. The results indicate that the models for all but the industry hypothesis, number of auditors, number of EDP auditors, and potential for disruption, were significant at the .01 level. The hypothesis for potential of disruption was significant at the .1 level. Each correlation value, for all but industry and number of internal auditors, was significant at the .1 level or better. Correlation coefficients are used to indicate the direction of the relationships being tested. The hypothesized directions also are summarized in table 6-1.

ENVIRONMENT HYPOTHESES

Industry. In the case of the industry variable, the largest number of adopters were in the finance, insurance, utilities, and manufacturing industries. The highest percentage of adopters in different industries included food, agricultural and retail industries. However, there was no general industry effect.

Agencies. Alternatively, the other environment hypothesis, H2, the impact of agencies was significant at the .001 level. It appears that the flow of information is one of the critical factors separating adopters and nonadopters.

Table 6-1

SUMMARY OF RESULTS&

Question	Correlation (t-value)	Prob of Pearson Chi-Square (Probability)	Sign on Hypothesis
H1 (Industry)	−0.018 (-0.368)	0.3539	+/−
H2 (Information Flow)	0.185 (3.583)***	0.0011	+
H3 (No. of Internal Auditors)	0.042 (0.787)	0.6178	+
H4 (No. of EDP Auditors)	0.012 (1.421)*	0.2101	+
H5 (Development Support)	0.241 (4.682)***	0.0000	+
H6 (Firm-wide Pressure)	0.282 (5.152)***	0.0000	+
H7 (Budgetary Pressures)	−0.145 (-3.057)***	0.0072	−
H8 (Reduction in Manpower)	0.184 (3.580)***	0.0002	+
H9 (Uncertainty in Improvement)	−0.148 (-3.058)***	0.0105	−
H10 (ES have been Successful)	0.213 (4.069)***	0.0000	+
H11 (Potential for Disruption)	−0.073 (-1.485)*	0.1004	−
H12 (Inexpensive Shells)	0.130 (2.529)**	0.0086	+

& Results using subjects' responses coded with 0 = not adopted in audit processes, 1=low adoption, medium adoption and high adoption into audit process.

* *Significant at the .1 level*
** *Significant at the .01 level*
*** *Significant at the .001 level*

ORGANIZATIONAL HYPOTHESES

Size. The model associated with the number of internal auditors (H3) was not significant. However, there seems to be a unique relationship between number of internal auditors and adoption of ES. The standardized deviates, summarized in table 6-2, indicate that the relationship between size and adoption of the technology seems to change when the number of auditors exceeds 100.

It is possible that the number of auditors was not significant because another phenomenon was involved. It is likely that, although there may be economies of scales as firms become larger, at a certain point, the number of auditors appears to inhibit the potential for change. Apparently, when internal auditor organizations (and possibly public auditor organizations) reach a certain size, then their ability or willingness to consider new innovations may decrease. A similar finding occurs for the relationship between adoption and number of EDP auditors (H4). This finding deserves further investigation.

Opportunity and Pressure. The hypotheses for opportunity and pressure yielded the strongest statistical results. H5, the existence of support, was the second most significant of all the questions. Thus, it appears that one of the critical variables in the adoption process is the availability of support to help potential adopters to develop the sys-

Table 6-2

NUMBER OF INTERNAL AUDITORS AND ADOPTION OF EXPERT SYSTEMS*

Number of Int. Auditors	Nonadopters	Adopters	Total
Under 25	0.1	−0.2	−0.0
25 to 50	0.1	−0.1	−0.0
50 to 100	0.3	−0.4	−0.1
Over 100	−0.7	1.0	0.3
Total	−0.2	0.4	0.1

Standard Deviates. Standardized deviates are computed as (observed-expected)/squareroot of (expected).

tems for their department.

H6, the existence of firmwide pressure, yielded the strongest statistical result. Firmwide pressure appears to provide substantial incentive for technology adoption.

Budgetary Pressures. The lack of budgetary pressures (H7) was found to be positively and statistically significantly related to the adoption of ES. If the department does not have the resources then apparently that interferes with technology adoption.

NATURE OF THE INNOVATION

The analysis of the data indicates that each of the four characteristics tested in this research was found to be statistically significant at the .1 level or better.

Economic Advantage. The ability of ES to provide economic advantage, in particular, reduce manpower, was expected to be positively related to the adoption of ES. The results in table 1 indicate H8 significant at the .0002 level.

Uncertainty. If there is uncertainty about the ability of the technology to improve the process then that would be negatively related to adoption. The results indicate that H9 is significant at the .01 level.

Success. If the ES adoption is uncertain to lead to a successful implementation, then we would anticipate that to be negatively related to the adoption of ES. H10 was found to be significant at the .0000 level.

Disruption. If the adoption of ES were expected to be disruptive of other departments, then we would anticipate that would inhibit the adoption of ES. H11 was found to be significant at the .1 level.

Required Commitment. H12, suggested that if the perceived required commitment of ES is relatively minor then the technology will be adopted. H12 was found to be significant at the .01 level.

Summary, Contributions and Extensions

This section briefly summarizes the chapter, elicits some of the contributions of the chapter and discusses some extensions of the research in this chapter.

SUMMARY OF FINDINGS

The results in this chapter were consistent with the theory elicited from the economics of diffusion and innovation. The results indicate that adoption of the expert systems technology among internal auditors is positively related to the number of EDP auditors, firmwide pressure to adopt expert systems, the existence of support for expert systems development, the perceived potential for reducing manpower, the perception of the success of expert systems, and the existence of tools that require only minor commitment to try out the technology. It is also positively related to the flow of information from the IIA. The existence of budgetary pressures, the uncertainty of the technology to improve the audit process and the potential for disruption of other activities in the firm are negatively correlated with adopters.

The number of auditors was found to have an interesting relationship with adoption of expert systems technology. Once internal audit departments begin to get large (measured here as greater than 100 internal auditors), the adoption of technology seems to be inhibited.

CONTRIBUTIONS

This chapter has a number of implications for future research.

First, this is the first large-scale study of the factors relating to expert systems adoption in a discipline requiring substantial judgment. Accordingly, this study can guide future studies of expert system and other technology adoption. Second, the data analysis employs a log linear model. That approach is useful here, since it captures the differences associated with the levels in the variables that are measured. This same approach can be used in the analysis of similar data. Third, this study is one of the few large scale studies of accountant technology adoption. Future research could focus on other types of technology used in accounting. The study of a portfolio of technologies could provide additional insight into adoption of technologies. Fourth, the research findings here are consistent with previous diffusion research. As a result, this research substantiates previous work and the use of the economics of diffusion in the analysis of ES diffusion. Fifth, each study necessarily concentrates on a selected set of issues, e.g., disruption of other departments. Additional research could focus on other aspects, such as investment variables.

This chapter is the first to investigate the diffusion of a technology in accounting and audit judgment. Thus, the results presented here form a basis for the study of the diffusion of other accounting and audit judgment support tools.

The research employed the previous literature of expert systems in auditing and the economics of diffusion and innovation to develop a survey instrument that was sent to over 3,000 internal auditor department heads. The respondents were placed into one of three categories: not familiar with expert systems; familiar with expert systems, but did not adopt in their audit process; and familiar with expert systems, and adopt in their audit process. The focus of this chapter was on the differences between the last two categories (nonadopters and adopters).

EXTENSIONS

The results of this chapter can be extended in a number of different ways. First, the study could be extended to other time periods, to determine if there were any differences in the adoption of ES technology. Such a study could focus on changing patterns of factors. Second, the adoption of alternative forms of AI activity, such as case-based reasoning, not present in audit applications during the period investigated, could be analyzed. Third, the study could be extended to other audit judgment support tools and technologies, such as CD/ROM. Comparisons could then be made between the patterns of factors associated with technology adoption. Fourth, alternative types of auditing environments, such as public accounting, could be investigated for adoption factors. It is likely that many of the same factors influencing internal auditor decisions on adopting audit judgment support, also influence external auditors. Fifth, an understanding of adoption of ES may be used to study diffusion of general judgment support.

LIMITATIONS

As noted in Kerlinger [1973, p. 414], "survey research has contributed much to the methodology of the social sciences." However, the primary limitations of this study derive from the methodology being a survey. For example, throughout we are measuring perceptions of internal auditors, not actual actions. We never actually "see" the adoption of a technology. It is assumed that if the survey respondent tells us they have adopted the technology, then they are treated as an adopter. Although there are a number of well-known limitations, surveys still provide an important method for accessing large populations of professionals.

Chapter 6 Appendix
Frequency Table Percentages

This appendix presents the frequency tables in percentage form.

H1. Industry (not presented ... 22 different industries were in the set of respondents)

H2. Information Flow from IIA (Percentages)

Scale	Nonadopters	Adopters	Total
−1	42.1	13.8	55.9
0	22.7	14.3	36.9
+1	3.4	3.7	7.1
Total	68.2	31.8	100.0

H3. Number of Auditors (Percentages)

Scale	Nonadopters	Adopters	Total
Under 25	52.0	23.6	75.6
25 to 50	8.4	3.7	12.1
50 to 100	3.9	1.5	5.4
Over 100	3.9	3.0	6.9
Total	68.2	31.8	100.0

H4. Number of EDP Auditors (Percentages)

Scale	Nonadopters	Adopters	Total
Under 10	61.3	27.3	88.7
10 to 25	5.2	2.5	7.6
Over 25	1.7	2.0	3.7
Total	68.2	31.8	100.0

H5. Support (Percentages)

Scale	Nonadopters	Adopters	Total
−1	47.0	13.5	60.6
0	18.0	15.0	33.0
+1	3.2	3.2	6.4
Total	68.2	31.8	100.0

H6. Organizational Pressure (Percentages)

Scale	Nonadopters	Adopters	Total
−1	53.9	17.0	70.9
0	14.3	13.5	27.8
+1	0.0	1.2	1.2
Total	68.2	31.8	100.0

H7. Budgetary Pressures (Percentages)

Scale	Nonadopters	Adopters	Total
−1	23.2	14.3	37.4
0	32.8	15.0	47.8
+1	12.3	2.5	14.8
Total	68.2	31.8	100.0

H8. Manpower (Percentages)

Scale	Nonadopters	Adopters	Total
−1	14.8	4.7	19.5
0	45.1	17.7	62.8
+1	8.4	9.4	17.7
Total	68.2	31.8	100.0

H9. Improve Audit Process (Percentages)

Scale	Nonadopters	Adopters	Total
−1	20.0	13.3	33.3
0	33.7	14.8	48.5
+1	14.5	3.7	18.2
Total	68.2	31.8	100.0

H10. Successful Expert Systems (Percentages)

Scale	Nonadopters	Adopters	Total
−1	16.7	4.9	21.7
0	48.5	20.4	69.0
+1	3.0	6.4	9.4
Total	68.2	31.8	100.0

H11. Disrupt the Organization (Percentages)

Scale	Nonadopters	Adopters	Total
−1	41.4	22.4	63.8
0	22.9	14.8	30.3
+1	3.9	2.0	5.9
Total	68.2	31.8	100.0

H12. Inexpensive Shells (Percentages)

Scale	Nonadopters	Adopters	Total
−1	17.2	6.4	23.6
0	42.1	17.2	59.2
+1	8.9	8.1	17.0
Total	68.2	31.8	100.0

References

Boritz, J., "CAPS: The Comprehensive Audit Planning System," Paper presented at the University of Southern California Symposium on Audit Judgment, 1983.

————, "Audit MASTERPLAN," Audit Planning Software Published by the Institute of Internal Auditors, 1986.

Brown, C. and Phillips, M., "Expert Systems for Internal Auditing," *Internal Auditor,* August 1991, pp. 23-28.

Burton, C., "Experts Say AI Freeze is Beginning to Thaw," *Computerworld,* July 29, 1991, p. 66.

Carlson, J., "Aspects of the Diffusion of Technology in the United States," Paper presented at the fifth meeting of the Senior Economic Advisors, United Nations, Economics Commission for Europe, Geneva, October 2, 1967.

Dixon, W., Brown, M., Engelman, L., Frane, J., Hill, M., Jennrich, R., Toporek, J., *BMDP Statistical Software Manual,* University of California Press, Berkley, Ca. 1988.

Flesher, D. and Martin, C., "Artificial Intelligence," *The Internal Auditor,* February, 1987, pp. 32-36.

Gold, B., "Industrial Growth Patterns: Theory and Empirical Findings," *Journal of Industrial Economics,* Volume 12, November 1964.

————, Peirce, W., and Rosegger, G., "Diffusion of Major Technological Innovations in U.S. Iron and Steel Manufacturing," *Journal of Industrial Economics,* Volume 18, July 1970.

————, "Diffusion of Technology in Industry," in *Research, Technological Change and Economic Analysis,* edited by B. Gold, Lexington, MA, D.C.Heath, Lexington Books, 1977.

Kennedy, C. and Thirlwall, A., "Surveys in Applied Economics: Technical Progress," *Economic Journal,* Volume 82, March 1972.

Kerlinger, F., *Foundations of Behavioral Research,* Holt, Rinehart, and Wilson, New York, 1983.

Lecot K., "An Expert System Approach to Fraud Prevention and Detection," *Expert Systems Review,* Volume 1, Number 3, 1988.

Mansfield, E., *Industrial Research and Technological Innovation,* New York, 1968.

Moeller, R., *Artificial Intelligence—A Primer,* Institute of Internal Auditors Monograph Series, 1987.

Ramakrishna, K., Dillard, J., Harrison, T., and Chandrasekaran, B., "An Intelligent Manual for Price Analysis," *Federal Acquisition Research Symposium,* U.S., Air Force, Willamsburg, Virgina, December 1983.

Rosegger, G., *The Economics of Production and Innovation,* Pergamon Press, Oxford, 1980.

Simon, H., "Technology and Environment," *Management Science,* Volume 19, June 1973.

Tener, W., "Expert Systems for Computer Security," *Expert Systems Review,* Volume 1, Number 2, March 1988.

Turban, E. and Watkins, P., "Integrating Expert Systems and Decision Support Systems," *Management Information Systems Quarterly,* June 1986, pp. 121-138.

Vasarhelyi, M., Halper, F., and Fritz, R., "The Continuous Audit of On-line Systems," Paper presented at the University of Southern California Audit Judgment Conference, 1988.

Williamson, M., "Knowledge-based Systems," *PC Week,* July 1990.

Chapter 7

THE IMPACT OF INFORMATION TECHNOLOGY ADOPTION ON STATUS:
An Exchange Theory Analysis of Expert Systems Adoption

Introduction

Economic factors are promulgated as the primary decision variables in the evaluation and adoption of new technologies (e.g., Rosegger [1980])). However, this Chapter finds that status also apparently is a major concern in such decisions.

Exchange theory (Blau [1964 and 1974] and others) was used as the basis of the formulation of hypotheses in this study. In exchange theory an actor increases their status, with respect to a reference group, when they make productive contributions to the group. Status is seen as a means of recognition of contributions to the group. Effectively individuals accrue status "capital" as they contribute to the group. The adoption of information technology has the potential to provide a number of contributions to the firms and groups within firms. As a result, exchange theory can be a useful tool to investigate general issues of information technology adoption and the resulting impact on those organizations, as they relate to such issues as status.

SUMMARY OF RESULTS

The results of this empirical study indicate that status is associated with a number of expert system adoption variables. Status is found to be statistically significant in an analysis that includes independent variables such as the estimation of perceptions of manpower reductions, process improvements, and the success of expert systems, in general. Status also is found to be statistically significant in conjunction with the adoption of expert systems technology.

Status, associated with the adoption of expert systems is not found to be statistically significant with budgetary pressures. This suggests that economic measures are not the only important bases of analysis. Instead researchers and practitioners need to consider status and variables that impact status.

IMPORTANCE OF THE PROBLEM

The relationship between status and technology evaluation and adoption is an important issue for a number of reasons. First, most research on technology adoption is economic (e.g., Rosegger [1980]), and ignores such issues as status. This chapter argues that status may be a critical variable in the evaluation and adoption of a technology.

Second, previous research has only provided a limited investigation of the relationship between status and technology adoption. There has been virtually no investigation of the relationship between status and expert systems or other types of artificial intelligence.

Third, internal auditors employ expert systems to assist them in complex decision problems. Thus, understanding the status associated with the adoption of a technology by internal auditors may facilitate understanding other groups of expert system adopters.

Fourth, expert systems generally are designed to support decision making. Thus, understanding the relationship between status and adoption of expert systems can also help in understanding decision support systems and possibly other information technologies.

PLAN OF THIS CHAPTER

This chapter proceeds as follows. The next section analyzes the impact of adopting expert systems from the perspective of exchange theory and summarizes these arguments as hypotheses. The subsequent section discusses the development of the questionnaire and the choice of the respondents. The following section presents the questions used in the questionnaire and a discussion of the methods used to analyze the responses. The next section briefly discusses the findings. The final section provides a brief summary and some extensions.

EXCHANGE THEORY, STATUS AND ADOPTION OF EXPERT SYSTEMS

The hypotheses were generated from exchange theory (e.g., Blau [1964]). The hypotheses are grouped into five different categories, for purposes of presentation: Reference Group Variables; Budgetary Constraints; Benefits; Information Flow; and Adoption of Technology. For each of the resulting hypotheses, "status" refers to the increase in status capital by adopting the use of expert systems technology.

REFERENCE GROUPS

Reference group is one of the most important aspects of exchange theory. As noted by Blau [1967, p. 158], "People belong to many groups, and potentially to still others, which constitute reference groups with which they compare themselves." In the case of internal auditors concerned with the adoption of technology such as expert systems, the direct reference groups are likely to be EDP auditors (auditors specializing in technology and the audit of technology) and the firm as a whole.

As noted by Blau [1964, pp. 53-55] "agreeing with others is a way of making oneself attractive to them." Status is achieved by adopting the opinions of the reference group. As a result, we would expect that firmwide pressure to adopt expert systems would have a positive impact on status associated with internal auditors adopting expert systems technology. Thus, we have the following hypothesis:

Hypothesis 1 (H1) (Q14i and Q13) (Pressure). Status is positively related to the firmwide pressure to adopt the use of expert systems.

In addition, we would expect the direct reference group to have more influence if it is larger than if it is smaller.

> There are fundamental differences between the dynamics of power in a collective situation and the power of one individual over another. The weakness of the isolated subordinate limits the significance of his approval or disapproval of the superior. The agreement that emerges in a collectivity of subordinates concerning their judgment of the superior on the other hand has far-reaching implications for developments in the social structure. (Blau [1964, p. 23])

As a result, we would expect the status associated with the adoption of expert systems to be larger if the reference group is larger. As a result, we have the following hypothesis.

107

Hypothesis 2 (H2) (Q14i and Q3b) (Number of EDP). Status is positively related to the number of EDP auditors.

BUDGETARY CONSTRAINTS

An important issue is the relationship between the status that accrues with the use and/or adoption of a technology and the direct budgetary impact. Blau [1964, p. 132] suggests that "Status can be considered capital, which an individual can draw on to obtain benefits, which is expended in use and which can be expanded profitably by investing it ..." Since status is considered a source of capital, this would suggest that status functions under its own 'budgetary' constraints, and does not rely on a monetary budget. This leads to the following hypothesis.

Hypothesis 3 (H3) (Q14i and Q14a) (Budget). Status is not related to budgetary pressures.

BENEFITS

Blau [1964, p. 47], noted that "Men who make essential contributions to a group as a whole, or its members individually, have an undeniable claim to superior status." In the case of internal auditing, such contributions from expert systems could include manpower reductions (H4), improvement of the audit process (H5) or perceived success of expert systems (H6). As a result, we have the following hypothesis:

Hypothesis 4 (H4) (Q14i and Q14c) (Manpower). Status is positively related to the perception of the ability of expert systems to reduce manpower needs.

Hypothesis 5 (H5) (Q14i and Q14d) (Improvement). Status is positively related to the perception of the ability of expert systems to improve the audit process.

Hypothesis 6 (H6) (Q14i and Q14e) (Success). Status is positively related to the perceived success of expert systems.

INFORMATION FLOW

The information flows that bring the information of the technology to the potential adopter is a critical issue. With no information flow, there is no information relating to the benefits and thus, no information to build status associated with the technology. Two of the primary organizations that can bring information to the internal auditor department heads regarding different technologies are the Institute of Internal Auditors (IIA) and the EDP Auditors Association (EDPAA). This leads to the following hypothesis.

Hypothesis 7 (H7) (Q14i and Q14g) (Information Flow). Status is positively related to the perceived information flow on the use of the expert systems received from IIA and the EDPAA.

The extent to which information flow is operationalized into formats for use in evaluation of the technology is also critical to adoption. One measure of information operationalization at this time was the cost of expert system shells. Expert system shells are software that can be used to speed the expert system development process. At the time of this questionnaire, rule-based systems for internal auditing purposes had been built or were under construction, by a number of firms, using inexpensive shells that cost around $300.

In addition, as noted by Blau [1974, p. 212], "A man who commands services others cannot do without ... can attain power over them by making the satisfaction of their needs contingent on their compliance with his directives." Thus, if the adopter has knowledge that others do not have, such as the tools of technology, including expert systems, then that adopter may derive status. Thus, we have the following hypothesis:

Hypothesis 8 (H8) (Q14i and 14h) (Suitability). Status is positively related to the perception of being able to build expert systems for use in internal auditing using inexpensive expert system shells (e.g., $300).

ADOPTION OF TECHNOLOGY

Ultimately, social exchange theory would argue that the technology would be adopted if that adoption were to have a substantial impact on the status capital of the adopter. Thus, because of the benefits of the technology, we would expect the following hypothesis.

Hypothesis 9 (H9) (Q14i and Q5) (Adopt/Non Adopt). Status is positively related to whether expert systems are adopted.

Questionnaire Analysis

Only a portion of the questionnaire was devoted to the study of status associated with expert systems technology in internal auditing.

QUESTIONS

The questions used in the questionnaire are summarized below. (The complete survey is in the appendix.) Average response and standard deviation are included here at the end of the question. The term "Qi" refers to the ith question.

The following question required a response from (-1 None, 0 Some, +1 Extensive)

Q13   Is there a firmwide "pressure" to adopt the use of expert systems technologies into departments within your firm, including internal auditing (–.7/.49)?

The following question required an assessment of the number of EDP auditors. Subjects were required to "fill in the blank."

Q3a   Please indicate the approximate number of employees in the EDP Audit Function (4.81/9.10).

The remainder of the questions required a choice of (–1 not true, 0, +1 true)

Q14a   Budgetary pressures make it impossible to spend any resources on expert systems in internal auditing (–.22/.69).

Q14c   Expert systems offer advantages in terms of reducing manpower needs over current manual methods (–.02/.61).

Q14d   There is substantial uncertainty that expert systems can improve the audit process (–.15/.7).

Q14e   Expert Systems developed to date have had very good success (–.12/.54).

Q14g   There has been substantial flow of information from organizations, such as the IIA and the EDPAA regarding the use of expert systems in accounting and auditing (–.48/.63).

Q14h   Suitable expert systems can be built for use in internal auditing using inexpensive (e.g., $300) expert system shells (–.067/.63).

Q5   To what extent are you employing expert systems technology as part of the internal audit function? (0 None, 1 Low, 2 Moderate, 3 High). (.4/.66). (Response of 1, 2, and 3 were aggregated together since it was assumed that a firm either adopted or did not adopt expert systems technology.)

Q14i   Expert systems in internal audit improve the status of internal auditors. (.02/.69)

ANALYSIS OF RESULTS

The approach was to use a model designed to study the relationship between the status variable and the variables associated with the responses for each of the questions 1 through 9. A log linear model was used to investigate the resulting frequency tables using BMDP (Dixon et al. [1981]). The frequency tables, by percentage in groups, are summarized in the appendix.

The quality of the model was measured using the Pearson ratio chi-square test. The Pearson correlation coefficient for the model was used for determination of direction, and its t-value was used to measure its significance.

Results

The results substantiate each of the hypotheses developed above. The results are summarized in tables 7-1 and 7-2.

The status variable analyzed results from question Q14i. The other variables that were analyzed were the categorical responses to the other questions. The results generated by the log linear model were used to substantiate the hypotheses.

Those results include the following. First, both the reference group responses (firmwide pressure and number of EDP auditors) were found to be positively and significantly related to the status variable.

Second, the budget variable was found to be unrelated to the status variable. It appears that the status and budget variables are unrelated in this data set.

Third, the benefits of expert systems were related to the status variable. Both the specific reduction of manpower and the general success of expert systems were also found to be strongly related to the status variable. Further, the existence of uncertainty of improvement using the technology was found to be negatively related to the status variable.

Each of the information flow variables also was related to the status variable. Finally, the adoption of the technology also was strongly related to the status variable.

Table 7-1

LOG LINEAR MODEL OF EXPERT SYSTEM ADOPTION
AND STATUS

Variable	Correlation Coefficient	t-value	Significance
Reference Group Variables			
H1-Number of EDP	0.103	2.431	.01
H2-Pressure	0.161	3.396	.001
Monetary Reference			
H3-Budget	0.019	0.378	***
Benefits			
H4-Manpower	0.247	4.737	.0001
H5-Improvement Uncertainty	−0.234	−4.514	.0001
H6-Success	0.177	3.384	.001
Information Flow			
H7-Information Flow	0.196	3.838	.001
H8-Suitability	0.189	3.374	.001
Adoption of Technology			
H9-Adopt/Non Adopt	0.121	2.456	.01

*** Greater than .1

Summary and Extensions

This chapter has investigated the relationship between status and adoption of an information technology. In particular, the chapter studied adoption of expert systems by internal auditors.

Status plays an important role in the "exchange theory" investigation of human behaviors. In exchange theory an actor increases their status, with respect to a reference group, when they make contributions to the group. Status is seen as a means of recognition of contributions to the group. Information technology can provide a number of contributions to the firms and groups within firms. As a result,

Table 7-2

LOG LINEAR MODEL OF EXPERT SYSTEM ADOPTION
AND STATUS*

Variable	Pearson Chi-Square	Significance/Degree of Freedom
Reference Group Variables		
H1-Number of EDP	8.826	.07 / 4
H2-Pressure	13.59	.01 / 4
Monetary Reference		
H3-Budget	0.570	.97 / 4
Benefits		
H4-Manpower	39.126	.00 / 4
H5-Improvement	29.951	.00 / 4
H6-Success	18.815	.01 / 4
Information Flow		
H7-Information Flow	18.243	.00 / 4
H8-Suitability	38.415	.00 / 4
Adoption of Technology		
H9-Adopt/Non Adopt	5.959	.05 / 2

* See Dixon et al. [1981] for detail on this approach.

exchange theory was used as the basis of the generation of the hypotheses and questionnaire questions.

The resulting questionnaire was sent to over 3000 internal department heads. A response rate of about 30% was obtained in the single mailing of questionnaires.

The results were consistent with the exchange theory-based hypotheses. The number of EDP auditors, the existence of firmwide pressure, benefits of manpower reduction, and the success of expert systems (in general) were all positively related to the status of internal auditors resulting from the adoption of expert systems. Budgetary pressures were not found to be related to the status associated with the adoption of expert systems. The existence of uncertainty in improvement resulting from the use of expert systems was negatively related to the status associated with the adoption of expert systems. Finally, status and adoption of the technology were strongly related.

The approach in this chapter could be generalized to other groups and other information or artificial intelligence technologies. In particular, the more general hypothesis, that the adoption of information technologies is done to improve status could be studied using other technologies, in other environments.

Appendix
Frequency Table Percentages

This appendix presents the frequency tables (in percentage form), analyzed using the log linear model presented in BMDP (Dixon et al. [1981]). In each case "status" (-1, 0, +1) is one of the two variables.

Status vs. Pressure

Scale	−1	0	1	Total
−1	19.5	36.2	15.3	70.9
0	3.2	15.5	9.1	27.8
+1	0.2	0.7	0.2	1.2
Total	22.9	52.5	24.6	100.0

Status vs. Number of EDP Auditors

Scale	−1	0	1	Total
Under 10	21.9	45.1	21.7	88.7
10 to 25	1.0	5.2	1.5	7.6
Over 25	0.0	2.2	1.5	3.7
Total	22.9	52.5	24.61	00.0

Status vs. Budget

Scale	−1	0	1	Total
−1	9.1	19.0	9.4	37.4
0	10.8	25.4	11.6	47.8
+1	3.0	8.1	3.7	14.8
Total	22.9	52.5	24.6	100.0

Status vs. Manpower

Scale	−1	0	1	Total
−1	6.4	9.4	3.7	19.5
0	15.0	36.0	11.8	62.8
+1	1.5	7.1	9.1	17.7
Total	22.9	52.5	24.6	100.0

Status vs. Uncertainty of Improvement

Scale	−1	0	1	Total
−1	5.2	15.8	12.3	33.3
0	10.3	28.8	9.44	8.5
+1	7.4	7.9	3.0	18.2
Total	22.9	52.5	24.6	100.0

Status vs. Uncertainty of Improvement

Scale	−1	0	1	Total
−1	5.2	15.8	12.3	33.3
0	10.3	28.8	9.4	48.5
+1	7.4	7.9	3.0	18.2
Total	22.9	52.5	24.6	100.0

Status vs. Success

Scale	−1	0	1	Total
−1	6.7	11.6	3.4	21.7
0	14.8	37.7	16.5	69.0
+1	1.5	3.2	4.7	9.4
Total	22.9	52.5	24.6	100.0

Status vs. Information Flow

Scale	−1	0	1	Total
−1	15.3	30.5	10.1	55.9
0	6.7	19.2	11.1	36.9
+1	1.0	2.7	3.4	7.1
Total	22.9	52.5	24.6	100.0

Status vs. Suitability

Scale	−1	0	1	Total
−1	8.6	10.6	4.4	23.6
0	10.3	36.7	12.3	59.2
+1	3.9	5.2	7.9	17.0
Total	22.9	52.5	24.6	100.0

Status vs. Adoption

Scale	−1	0	1	Total
Nonadopt	17.5	36	14.8	68.2
Adopt	5.4	16.5	9.9	31.8
Total	22.9	52.5	24.6	100.0

References

Blau, P., *Exchange and Power in Social Life,* John Wiley and Sons, New York, 1964.

————., *On the Nature of Organizations,* Wiley, New York, 1974.

Burton, C., "Experts Say AI Freeze is Beginning to Thaw," *Computerworld,* July 29, 1991, p. 66.

Dixon, W., Brown, M., Engelman, L., Frane, J., Hill, M., Jennrich, R., Toporek, J., *BMDP Statistical Software 1981,* University of California Press, Berkley, Ca 1981.

Hayes-Roth, F., Waterman, D., and Lenat, D., *Building Expert Systems,* Addison-Wesley, Reading, Massachusetts, 1983.

O'Leary, D. and Watkins, P., "Expert Systems and Decision Support Systems in Auditing," *Expert Systems Review,* 1989, pp. 3-22.

Rosegger, G., *The Economics of Production and Innovation,* Pergamon Press, Oxford, 1980.

Tener, W., "Expert Systems for Computer Security," *Expert Systems Review,* Volume 1, Number 2, March 1988.

Williamson, M., "Knowledge-based Systems," *PC Week,* July 1990.

Chapter 8

AUDIT, SECURITY, AND CONTROL ISSUES OF EXPERT SYSTEMS*

Issues in the Auditing of Expert Systems

Accounting researchers and systems developers have been working with artificial intelligence and expert systems for almost ten years (e.g., Michaelson [1982]). During that time, accounting and auditing expert systems have gone from the lab to the field. Now expert systems are available to auditors, e.g., LOANPROBE (Ribar [1988]). In addition, auditors are now in an environment where not only can they use expert systems, but also their clients use expert systems, e.g., Davis [1987]. It is these two developments that suggest that auditing those expert systems is now an important issue.

Unfortunately, there has been limited research and experience on the auditing of those expert systems. This neglect could have severe consequences. As noted by Moeller [1988, p. 8], "One would hope that we will not have to wait for an 'Equity Funding' type of event covering an expert system in order to have the impetus for sufficient audit guidance materials." Thus, the purpose of this Chapter is to investigate some of the primary issues in the auditing of expert systems. It does that by first reviewing previous research and then exploiting the unique characteristics of expert systems for audit purposes.

This chapter of the book first considers some of the unique characteristics of expert systems which differentiates expert systems from

---

*An earlier version of this chapter was published by the AICPA Information Technology Division as "Audit and Security Issues with Expert Systems."

119

other computer systems. The focus is on isolating those unique aspects of expert systems and investigating potential audit activity in order to meet the needs of those unique characteristics.

Second, the previous research on auditing expert systems is reviewed. Third, the types of expert systems applications that require audit is analyzed. Fourth, the differences resulting from the nature of the integration of expert systems with other traditional systems is addressed. Fifth, the requirements that expert systems suggest for the composition of the audit team is analyzed. Sixth, the impact which the attitude of the firm or department or activity being audited has, regarding expert systems is discussed. Finally, techniques of verification and validation of expert systems in order to determine the quality of the system are reviewed.

UNIQUE CHARACTERISTICS OF EXPERT SYSTEMS

Expert Systems and artificially intelligent systems are substantially different than traditional computer systems. As a result of these differences, it becomes necessary to address the implications for auditing these systems. Since the audit of traditional systems has been the subject of many books and papers, it is not the purpose here to repeat those analyses. Instead, the concern is only with those aspects which indicate audit differences from traditional computer–based systems. In order to investigate those differences in audit procedures, some of the differences between traditional computer programs, and expert systems and other intelligent systems are reviewed.

EXPERT SYSTEM DEVELOPMENT

In many cases the development of expert systems is done by domain experts or users, not by a systems development department engineer. For example, DuPont's well-known approach is to have a large number of expert systems developed by individual users. Since the systems development department is not included in the process those systems are not likely to be developed with the same formality and structure. In addition, there is no generally accepted model of an expert systems life cycle or development methodology. Thus, it often is impossible for the auditor to achieve comfort regarding the quality of the system, based on the development process. As a result, more emphasis generally is given to the testing of the system to ensure its quality. Tests of system quality generally are referred to as validation and verification tests.

DELIVERY ENVIRONMENT

Since the user is often the developer, the personal computer (PC) becomes the development and delivery environment. In other situations, the system is directly designed for use on a PC. In either of those circumstances the extent of use of the systems is difficult to control. Systems can be developed and play an integral part in decision making without the auditor being aware of the existence of the application. The easy replication of PC software provides an additional concern. Even if the auditor is associated with the development of a system, that does not guarantee that there is control over the extent to which the system will be duplicated and used by others.

SYMBOLIC VS. NUMERIC

Traditional computer programs typically process numeric data contained in databases. Expert Systems and intelligent systems process knowledge in the form of rules and numeric data (database information and certainty factors on the rules). In the case of numeric databases there is software that allows the auditor to investigate relationships in the data. For the case of expert systems, there is no similar tool other than the expert shell in which the system is developed, to assist in the examination of the knowledge.

PROBLEMS: WELL-STRUCTURE VS. NOT-YET-STRUCTURED

Most traditional computer programs are designed to solve well-structured problems, that previously often have been structured as computer programs. For example, accounting programs, such as accounts payable and accounts receivable, are well-established applications.

On the other hand, most expert systems are designed for decision problems that are not yet structured or difficult to structure problems. Previous versions of solution approaches could include checklists or documentation or may have no written structure. The lack of previous models can make the validation process a complicated one.

SPECIAL FIXES

Typically, a fraction of the knowledge (less than 10%) escapes standard representation schemes and requires special fixes (Fox [1979]), which can take any one of numerous designs. They may be ambiguous terminology or well-structured modules, such as linear programming modules. In any case, special fixes provide an opportunity to hide knowledge that can result in unusual or dysfunctional behavior.

EXPERT SYSTEMS EMULATE HUMAN BEHAVIOR

Since expert systems emulate human problem solving behavior the reaction of users to the embodiment of the expertise in a computer program may be a critical variable. For example, in one system discussed in Chapter 4, users began to assume that the expert system would do all of the same things that the humans it replaced would do. Unfortunately, the system was only designed to do certain functions, and the remaining humans were expected to do other functions for which the system was not designed. As a result, some functions were not done, the users thought that "the system will do that."

PREVIOUS RESEARCH

There has been limited direct reference to auditing expert systems. However, there have been at least three papers and one discussion from a book on EDP Auditing, that address issues on auditing expert systems.

Moeller [1993] related the audit of expert systems with existing audit literature, including a discussion of the relationship of SAS's #3, 48 and 55 to the internal control structure of expert systems. As part of his discussion, Moeller [1993, p. 236] notes that "While there is a growing body of other literature covering the auditor's use of expert systems, there is very little published material on audit techniques for reviewing expert systems."

Moeller's [1993] perspective is that auditing of expert systems should be aimed primarily at those expert systems in "financially significant applications." This approach was suggested since the role of the auditor is to attest that the financial statements are fairly stated.

In order to meet the unique requirements of expert systems, Moeller [1988] suggests that the audit of expert systems can be accomplished using "conventional application control procedures." In particular, control analysis was provided using input controls, processing controls and output controls.

Kick [1989] discussed some of the risk exposures associated with expert systems resulting from loss of strategic or competitive position, inability to sustain growth and loss of strategic knowledge. Kick's [1989, p. 35] primary emphasis was on ensuring that the auditor examine expert systems applications to determine if they are properly applied; deployed to gain strategic advantage, cost-effective; well-designed and operationally efficient; minimize exposure to fraud, poor decision making and other consequences; users are properly trained; and that the expert systems are "easy to maintain and continually updated.

In order to accommodate those concerns Kick suggested audit procedures that consisted of the following steps: examine selection priorities; review development standards; define roles and identify risks; review knowledge engineering and validation process; evaluate efficiency and effectiveness; and evaluate the maintenance history.

Jamieson [1993] presented an analysis of the audit of expert systems. In that research he identified a number of objectives: identify the personnel relevant to an audit investigation; identify the developer of the system; present an expert system development life cycle; review the evaluation of expert systems; understand the security, control and auditability requirements appropriate for an expert system environment; review those mechanisms; understand where auditors should be involved in the development process; and review documentation and legal concerns associated with expert system development. Jamieson [1993] treats the issue of auditing expert systems in the context of traditional systems and the components of an expert system (knowledge base, etc.).

Watne and Turney [1990] briefly analyze expert systems as a target of the audit. Watne and Turney [1990] suggest that systems that directly impact the balances in the financial statements or systems that provide information to the auditor each be the potential target of audits. They also analyze some of the controls in expert systems using a structure based on general controls and application controls. Watne and Turney also note that the computer science area of validation (e.g., O'Leary [1987]) is the source of tests for the reliability and quality of the expert systems.

WHAT TYPES OF SYSTEMS NEED TO BE AUDITED?

A critical issue in the development of an expert system is what systems need to be audited. As with traditional systems, those systems that impact the financial statements in a material manner require audit. However, since the systems emulate human expertise they can have a far-reaching impact on the auditor and the firm. Thus, there are at least four basic types of systems that need to be audited that are identified in this report:

1. systems that impact the financial statements (Moeller [1993] and Watne and Turney [1990]),

2. systems that may impact the going concern status of the firm,

3. systems that provide the auditor information that is relied on in an audit, (Watne and Turney [1990]) and

4. systems where efficiency and effectiveness are an issue of concern to the auditor (Kicks [1989]).

SYSTEMS THAT IMPACT THE FINANCIAL STATEMENTS

In some cases it will be found that the system will impact the financial statements directly. This can occur in at least two different ways. First, system activity may directly impact a particular account, such as loans. Second, the system may perform the tasks of a human accountant, such as allocating costs and revenues to different accounts.

In the first case, a system designed to assist in the choice of whom banks lend to can directly impact the quality of the loans by the bank. Further, in the case of authorizing credit card transactions, the authorization will impact the financial statements. A broad base of other expert systems also impact the financial statements.

In the second case, the expert system may provide or manipulate accounting numbers in the same way as a human would manipulate the numbers. In this situation, the program could include intelligence that leads it to make some inappropriate allocations. For example, revenues could be allocated to different periods in order to ensure a smoothness of income.

In each of the two cases, the materiality of the activity would be a concern. If the levels were immaterial and the potential for fraud minimal then further audit would not necessarily be cost-beneficial.

SYSTEMS THAT CAN IMPACT THE GOING CONCERN STATUS OF THE FIRM

Many expert systems that are developed will not directly impact the financial statements, but should be audited nevertheless. These systems include those whose activity is critical to the particular firm to the extent that its failure could force a change in the going concern status of that firm. Such status change is a definite concern for the auditor.

For example, consider the situation of Van de Kamps (LA Times, September 12, 1990) where a new computer system disrupted deliveries to the point where the firm was reportedly forced into bankruptcy. Although Van de Kamps is a privately held firm and the system that was implemented does not necessarily suggest an expert system, it does demonstrate the far reaching impact that a computer system can have.

SYSTEMS THAT IMPACT THE AUDIT

The growing use of expert systems in the audit process has been discussed by a number of researchers (e.g., O'Leary and Watkins [1989]). If expert systems are used in the audit process then those systems themselves should be audited. These systems may be either the external auditor's systems or internal auditor systems on which the external auditor relies.

SYSTEM EFFICIENCY AND EFFECTIVENESS

Once an expert system is developed and found to provide correct decisions, then concern may turn to alternative issues, such as the efficiency and effectiveness of the system. There are a number of those issues and a methodology to evaluate their importance.

INTEGRATION OF EXPERT SYSTEMS

Since there are a number of reasons to expect that expert systems are different than other computer systems, the integration of expert systems with traditional computer systems deserves additional consideration. The previous research has exhibited very different views on the impact that integration has on both what is audited and when it requires auditing. Kick [1989, p. 35] has suggested that "... a system that is embedded in an accounts receivable application should be audited as a separate entity and not merely as a component of the accounts receivable system." While, Moeller [1993, p. 238] gives the following example:

> ... (the) American Express expert system works under or is part of a much larger overall credit authorization system, a conventionally programmed application. While audit attention has almost certainly been given to that overall authorization system, it would not necessarily be given to the Authorizer Assistant subsystem. The auditor would give consideration to that subsystem only if it controlled a material amount of the receivable balances.

INTEGRATION OF SYSTEMS AND WORK PROCESSES

The classic expert system is a stand-alone system that is designed to solve a single problem or part of a problem. However, in the evolution of expert systems they have begun to be integrated into other traditional computer systems. Thus, an important issue in the audit of an expert system is the extent to which the system is integrated with other systems or work processes. This set of structures is illustrated in Figure 8-1.

Figure 8-1

INTEGRATION OF SYSTEMS IN PROCESSES

	Stand-Alone Probem	Integrated Problem
Stand-Alone System	A	B
Integrated System	C	D

IMPACT ON AUDIT

For systems of type A, the audit of the system can be decomposed from much of the rest of the firm for independent assessment. Systems in this category might include a loan approval system, where much of the activity for each system and use of each system is relatively independent from other purposes and users.

However, for systems in categories B, C and D, the expert system is part of a system. It interacts with other components of the system. As such, concern should be with the expert system as a component, as it interacts with the rest of the system components or work processes and the overall system.

Systems in category B are distinguished from those in category A by the extent to which the system completes work on the problem. If the system only provides a solution for a part of the problem then there are a number of other systems or persons with which the system must interface.

Systems in categories C and D are the more difficult situations since the system is integrated with another system and possibly is only a portion of the work process. The integration with another system means that inputs or outputs or both are sent between the system and another system. Such interaction of systems can complicate the audit of the expert system component since the two systems likely employ different technologies.

The impact of integration can be further complicated by the nature of the other system. For example, if the other system is an accounting database from which the accounting financial statements are constructed, then audit becomes even more critical.

In any case, the primary concern should be the audit of the system. This implies that any expert system component be audited. In addition, it also indicates that the system as a whole be audited. By saying that a component does not need audit if it does not include a material level of activity, suggests that if the components are made small enough no system will ever have sufficient materiality to require audit.

SOURCE OF SYSTEM DEVELOPMENT

As with other computer systems, expert systems can be developed or they can be purchased. As noted earlier, experts and users of systems provide a unique set of concerns in the development and use of expert systems, particularly when implemented in a PC environment.

As noted by Jamieson [1993, p. 253], the dangers of user developed expert systems include "... inadequate documentation, lack of concern for security, control and audit matters, poor knowledge based programming and little testing and formal evaluation of knowledge bases." Similar concerns arise for systems developed in other environments, including those systems developed in research labs. Typically, to the auditor, this means that more testing of the systems is required. However, there are additional potential concerns associated with user developed systems, including determining the existence and extent of use of such systems.

FINDING THE SYSTEMS

Systems developed by research labs or systems development departments or systems purchased by the firm often leave a clear trace of their existence and use. However, user developed systems do not leave such a trace of their existence. Although user developed expert systems may be embedded in decision processes in a PC environment, the presence of the systems on a PC environment does not automatically make those applications immaterial. Instead, PC-based systems may have a material impact on decisions. As a result, the auditor should take steps to identify the existence of these systems.

USE OF THE SYSTEMS

Oftentimes useful PC-based systems are passed from one decision maker to another, because of the ease with which they are copied and implemented on an alternative PC. As a result, multiple copies of the system maybe located throughout the firm. If that is the case then the materiality may not be dependent on the single copy identified by the auditor. Thus, the existence of such additional copies should be investigated.

NATURE OF THE AUDITOR TEAM

The audit of expert systems requires both knowledge of expert systems technology and knowledge of the domain in which the system is built.

NEED FOR DOMAIN KNOWLEDGE

Typically, in the development of an expert system, the developers become "near experts." There is substantial case evidence indicating that in those situations were the developers are not near experts at the beginning of the development process they are by the end of the process. For example, in Lethan and Jacobsen [1987] in order for the knowledge engineers to build a value added tax expert system they found it necessary to travel with the VAT accountants for over a year. Similarly, if the auditor does not have a knowledge of the domain on which a system is built then it would be very difficult for the auditor to assess the quality or correctness of the knowledge used in the expert system.

NEED FOR KNOWLEDGE REPRESENTATION KNOWLEDGE

Unlike the database systems where there is substantial computer software to assist the auditor in analyzing the database, there or no such software to assist with the analysis of knowledge bases.

If the auditor does not have a knowledge of knowledge representation and expert systems, then it would be very difficult for the auditor to assess the quality or correctness of the knowledge representation. In addition, it could prove very difficult for the expert to investigate issues such as efficiency and effectiveness of the system, if the auditor is unfamiliar with the technology.

ATTITUDE TOWARDS EXPERT SYSTEMS

As noted earlier, expert systems emulate human behavior. The very name expert system draws an analogy between a human and the computer program. As a result, users of the system or interfacers with the system may assume that the system is more than just a computer program. In Chapter 4 it was found that for one expert system embedded in a work process of other computer programs and people, there was ambiguity about what the computer program did and what it did not do. Those that interfaced with the system assumed that since it was an expert system that it was as thorough and complete as a human would be. Instead, the system was specialized to a specific domain and those humans that interfaced with it were expected to do some of the activities that the humans assumed that the system would do.

This also provides further evidence of the importance of not just treating the expert system as an independent entity, but instead viewing the system as a whole.

TECHNIQUES OF VALIDATION AND VERIFICATION

The unique aspects of expert systems discussed earlier indicate that in many cases the auditor will need to test the quality of the expert system. In addition, probably the most critical aspect of the auditing process is the examination of specific expert systems with concern for whether the knowledge in the knowledge base is in a correct form (verification) and whether the system makes correct judgments (validation). Verification has been referred to as ensuring that the system is correctly developed, while validation has been referred to as building the correct system. For more details of these kinds of systems, the reader is referred to the extensive list of references and the references in those papers.

There has been substantial research on verification and validation in the computer science literature, from which this discussion draws. However, not all the issues of verification and validation have been resolved. As a result, although some solutions are presented, future research may provide alternative and additional solution procedures.

VERIFICATION (NAZARETH [1989], NYGUYEN [1987] AND O'LEARY [1990A AND 1990B])

Verification examines whether the knowledge representation is correct. Probably the most frequently used form of knowledge representation is rules of the form "if a then b, with certainty factor y." If we assume that the knowledge is represented in the form of rules then some of the verification tests can be specified.

Nyguyen et al. [1987] and Nazareth [1989] provide tests that can be used to determine when rules are incorrect, incomplete, redundant and inconsistent. The rules are incorrect if there is circular reasoning in the rules, as in the following example: "if a then b"; "if b then c"; "if c then a." The rules are incomplete if there is a rule with no "a" or "b." There is redundancy if there are multiple versions of the same rule in the same knowledge base. The rules are inconsistent if there are two rules such as the following: "if a then b" and "if a then c". In this last case, the occurrence of "a" leads to b and c, yet it is unclear which should be used.

O'Leary [1990a] provides an analysis of potential problems with the representation of uncertainty factors in expert systems. O'Leary finds that developers of expert systems have difficulties using some of the schemas that have been developed to weigh the importance of the rules in an expert system. As a result, there are oftentimes weights that do not meet the underlying assumptions of probability theory.

There also have been verification approaches developed for additional forms of knowledge representation. For example, O'Leary [1990b] presents approaches for verification of frames and semantic networks.

VALIDATION (O'LEARY [1987, 1988b])

Validation is more concerned with the quality of the decisions of the expert system. There are a number of approaches to assist the auditor in the analysis of the validity of the system.

One of the most frequently used approaches is direct inspection of the knowledge by the expert. This is an approach that could benefit from the development of a system that facilitates examination of the knowledge, in the same way that audit software has been developed to assist in the examination of a database. Such software could allow the user to get a listing of the rules, get a pictorial network representation of the rules to assist in understanding how different rules are connected to each other.

The system can be treated as a black box and tested against human experts. In this test, the only concern would be the similarity of the judgments generated by the system and the judgments generated by the human expert. Typically, another human is used to compare the judgments to determine which is preferred.

An alternative to this last approach is to open up the system to understand why the system made certain judgments. In this case the explanation process plays a critical part in the process.

Unfortunately, all of these methods require substantial human involvement. As a result, there has been a movement to develop alternative methods, that require less direct human involvement. For example, O'Leary and Kandelin [1988] present statistical methods based on the weights on the rules in the expert system.

CONCLUSIONS—ISSUES IN AUDITING EXPERT SYSTEMS

Some of the key issues in the audit of expert systems have been identified. Throughout, the analysis was based on those unique aspects of expert systems that differentiate them from other traditional forms of knowledge representation. Previous research has focused on some of the issues in the audit of expert systems. However, additional issues were identified and some of the research of previous researchers was summarized.

The issues examined here included the following:

- The types of systems that need to be audited,

- The impact of integration of expert systems on auditing of those systems

- The impact on the source of system development,

- The nature of the auditor team,

- The attitude toward expert systems, and

- Techniques of verification and validation of expert systems.

ISSUES IN THE SECURITY OF EXPERT SYSTEMS

Typically, expert systems are computer programs with certain amounts of expertise or knowledge, derived from human sources. Those programs are then used by a decision maker to assist in decision making process. In some cases, the systems function independently of a human user, however, such systems are rare.

Most systems are developed using expert systems software referred to as an expert system shell. That software facilitates the development of representations of the knowledge gathered from experts. For example, the ES shell could help the developer design rules in which the knowledge would be stored (e.g. "If condition N then consequence Q"). Those rules sometimes include a weight representing the "strength of association" or probability of the statement. Shells also contain an inference engine that sorts through the knowledge in order to find the answers to user inquiries.

ES also sometimes interface with databases. These systems could derive data from these databases to assist in the development of answers to user inquiries. Alternatively, the users may be responsible for providing the data.

A critical issue to the initial and ongoing success of these expert systems is the security of the system. If the ES is not secure then the system is vulnerable to loss of assets (possibly in the particular application domain, e.g., accounting or loss of knowledge to competitors). In addition, if it is not secure it is also vulnerable to a loss of system credibility (in the system could be changed and the system would not function appropriately). In addition, there are other reasons for ensuring the security of the system, some of which are discussed latter in this paper. The purpose of this paper is to investigate some of the security issues in expert systems.

Since ES are computer programs they require the same security measures as other computer programs. Many of those concerns have been addressed in other sources (Halper et. al [1985] and Weber [1988]), and, thus, are beyond the scope of this paper. However, ES are different types of computer programs than other more traditional accounting computer programs, as discussed below. It is these differences that require the investigation of the security of these programs. Thus, the approach is to elicit some of the unique risks associated with expert systems and the knowledge in expert systems and then discuss some of the controls that could mitigate those risks.

Unique Characteristics of Expert Systems

ES are computer programs and need to be treated as other computer programs. However, there are a number of unique characteristics of ES that differentiate them from other computer programs, that create new security risks. These unique characteristics include:

- Development Methodology
- Maintenance Methodology
- Existence of Symbolic and Numeric
- Information
- Explanation of Knowledge
- Personal Computer Environment
- User Interface
- Downward Delegation
- Source of the Data
- Programming Software Limitations

The uniqueness deriving from each of these characteristics relates to the knowledge in the ES, and it is that knowledge that differentiates ES from other computer programs. That knowledge may be derived from human experts or proprietary questionnaires or books. In any case that knowledge is likely to be a valuable asset of the firm for which the system is built. Therefore, it is necessary to ensure that there are appropriate controls for the security of that knowledge. These controls include

- Control over the entry of knowledge to the system
- Access to that knowledge for either changing that knowledge or leakage of that knowledge
- Solicitation of data that leads to the system to use the wrong knowledge
- Software limitations allowing knowledge to access databases
- Use of knowledge to camouflage other uses of that knowledge (e.g., Trojan horses—programs disguised as other programs)

Controls are developed to mitigate these unique security risks.

DEVELOPMENT METHODOLOGY

ES normally are developed using a "middle-out" approach, also referred to as a prototyping approach (e.g., O'Leary [1988a]). Successive versions of the system iteratively are developed as the problem becomes better understood. In fact, the prototype assists in developing a better understanding so that another version of the system can be developed. This approach allows the developer to gradually determine the necessary knowledge for the system. This is in contrast to more traditional software engineering approaches such as a "top-down" or "bottom-up" approach.

Although prototyping has been found to be an excellent method for eliciting knowledge and gradually structuring the decision problem, it does introduce some security concerns. Researchers have found that prototyping makes managing and controlling the system development process difficult. If managing the process is more difficult, then it may also be more difficult to maintain security and easier for someone to sabotage the system.

MAINTENANCE METHODOLOGY

The maintenance of the knowledge base of an expert system raises a number of other issues, including "Who can update the knowledge in the system?" and "How is that updating process accomplished?"

The security of a system can be jeopardized if naive users are responsible for updating the system. Although, it is often suggested that knowledge can be freely entered and removed without disturbing the system, knowledge bases are fragile. The technical nature of the relationship between pieces of knowledge can be delicate, and easily disrupted by naive users, without appropriate knowledge maintenance equipment.

SYMBOLIC AND NUMERIC INFORMATION

ES process both symbolic information and numeric information. Knowledge may be represented, for example in a rule-based format ("if condition a then consequence b") and those rules may include "strengths of evidence" or probability assessments.

Traditional computer programs process only data. In ES security efforts can not be aimed at a single type of information, say numeric data. In addition, since other types of computer programs do not contain knowledge used as data by the program, there has been no previous investigation of how to secure that knowledge, the costs of not securing it, and a variety of other concerns.

EXPLANATION OF KNOWLEDGE TO THE USER

ES frequently provide the user with an "explanation" of the reasoning behind the decisions of the ES. That explanation can range from a "trace" of the sequence of rules that were used to come to the conclusions, to specially developed explanation systems. These explanations are "windows" to the insights of experts from whom the knowledge has been gathered.

Although insight into how the program gets to a decision may be important to a decision maker. Such insights may be used against the system. In the case of a system designed to assist in stock purchases, buy and sell rules could be discovered and used against the system. In the case of an audit system, insight into what transactions the system chooses to audit can be used against the system. Thus, the security of this area is another critical point in an ES.

PERSONAL COMPUTER ENVIRONMENT

ES are most often implemented in a personal computer (PC) like environment. PCs can be taken almost everywhere and generally are easy to use. As a result, many ES that interface directly with users are developed for a PC environment. This is probably because most of the development software has, until recently, been designed for workstations and PC's. In addition, much of the development of ES's is by those in the domain areas, whose easiest access to computing power is often through the PC.

As a result, ES developed for PC environments generally are developed for PC operating systems, which have few security devises. In addition, access controls in PC's generally are severely lacking.

USER INTERFACES

Typically, ES have friendly user interfaces. With these natural language and menu driven interfaces, as a result, unauthorized users may gain access to systems with only limited knowledge.

SOURCE OF DATA

ES will either solicit information directly from the user or from a database or both. Most traditional computer programs function independently of the user. Thus, data is massaged and numerous steps are taken to ensure that it is correct.

However, when data is solicited directly from the user there is substantial potential for error in that data. Humans make errors of omission, misinterpretation, inconsistency and other errors. If there is error on input to the system then the ES will use the wrong knowledge and could develop wrong recommendations.

DOWNWARD DELEGATION—DATABASE ACCESS

ES allow the leveraging of expertise. Thus, ES are used to "delegate" decision making downward. This can lead to situations where the ES needs access to data for which the user of the system may not have appropriate clearance. That is, the ES may have a higher priority than the user. As a result, either authorized or unauthorized access to the ES can yield unauthorized access to the database, and result in security problems.

PROGRAMMING SOFTWARE LIMITATIONS

As noted by researchers, e.g., Fox [1979], a portion of knowledge (typically less than 10%) escapes standard representation schemes and requires "special fixes." These special fixes can take any of a number of designs. For example, in order to accommodate non rule-based knowledge representation in a rule-based expert system shell, an external program or module could be used. In addition, a linear programming module or statistical module could be used to supplement or interface with the system.

Special fixes pose a security risk since they offer the opportunity to hide knowledge that can result in unusual or dysfunctional behavior. Such additional modules offer the potential for intruders to hide Trojan horse programs.

Controls for Expert Systems

Some controls can be used with all types of expert systems and all types of expert system software shells. These controls relate to general ES application development, ES program maintenance, ES relationships to databases, and organization of expert systems efforts.

DEVELOPMENT METHODOLOGY

The controls developed for the development methodology are those security measures designed to prevent and detect inappropriate or wrong knowledge from being entered into initial versions of the system. Although prototyping provides insights into the knowledge required for the problem solving process, as noted earlier there may be management and thus, security problems with the use of prototyping. Recently, some researchers have suggested a more traditional software engineering approach be used to develop expert systems (e.g., Bull et. al [1987]). As the number of expert systems developed increases and the size of those systems increases controls such as production schedules and quality assurance become critical to project management. In addition, as an increasingly larger number of people become involved in the development of expert systems the possibility of security problems increases.

MAINTENANCE METHODOLOGY

The security of the maintenance of an expert system is accomplished, in part, using organizational controls. The primary organizational response that has developed for expert systems is that of the role of the expert systems manager—ESM (e.g., see Section II of this report for the interview of the "Information Services" company). The ESM is responsible for the overall operation and maintenance of a given ES. Conceptually, the ESM is similar to the database administrator (e.g. Weber [1988]). ESM allows for assignment of responsibility, unlike team-based approaches where responsibility is difficult to assign.

An important maintenance approach built into some ES shells and specific systems are verification tests. Verification tests are controls on the quality of the data entered into particular ES systems. For example, these verification tests may be designed to ensure that there is no circular reasoning (If a then b; if b then c; if c then a) and a number of other tests. At this point the verification tests vary from shell to shell and from ES to ES. Nazereth [1989] surveys a number of these tests for rule-based systems.

In some large ES it may be cost beneficial to develop a specific system to assist in the updating and maintenance process. For example, in the case of EXPERTAX, a special maintenance system has been developed to assist in the process of updating the knowledge in that system (Shatz et. al [1987]).

SYMBOLIC AND NUMERIC INFORMATION (PREVENT/DETECT CHANGING KNOWLEDGE)

The literature of expert systems has ignored the development of specific tests that can be used to prevent and detect changing either the rules or the weights on the rules.

One preventive approach is to only provide the user with a run-time version of the system. However, in some cases, the user may need or receive a version of the system that is not a run-time version. For example, the software may not allow the development of run-time versions.

In these cases, alternative approaches can be used. For example, in the case of weights on rules, each weight could be multiplied times the number of the rule, a prime number or some other approach. An unauthorized change of a weight(s) would result in a change to that sum.

In the case of rules, some controls could be numeric in nature. For example, the number of rules, the sum of the number of words in a rule times the rule number or some other number would provide a detective basis for control on system changes.

Other traditional approaches such as base case testing could be used to detect the possibility of a change. Unfortunately, unless the test data tested the portion of the knowledge that was changed that approach may not work.

EXPLANATION OF KNOWLEDGE (PREVENT LEAKAGE OF KNOWLEDGE)

Two different controls are found in some types of ES shells. First, some shells offer the user the opportunity to provide an explanation different than the actual rules used by the system. This has the advantage of providing control over what is shown to the user of the ES and may be used to make the system easier to understand, since explanations rather than system knowledge are presented to the user. Second, in those cases where the explanations are different than the actual system knowledge, a "run-time" version can be used to control access to the knowledge. (A "run time" version is a compiled version of the system—a version not human readable.)

PERSONAL COMPUTER ENVIRONMENT

The personal computer environment has a number of security threats associated with it. The PC environment impacts any PC application. Since so many ES applications are on PCs, this environment is subjected to scrutiny here. First, the PC operating systems such as DOS have few security devises built into it. For example, there is no general capability such as passwords. Thus, if such devises as passwords are not added into general development ES efforts then they will not be available for use.

Second, most PCs are out in the open and easily accessed. Although locks on systems are available, they seldom are used. Further, in some cases the only access control to PCs is that they are locked in offices. Such easy access to PC, combined with easy to use interfaces, yields a situation with easy access to knowledge.

Third, PCs often are brought out of the office on location. Security of the expert system and other systems on the PC can improve if the hard disk or diskettes are brought with the user whenever the user would leave the system.

USER INTERFACE

One approach to developing secure user interfaces is to allow the use of passwords. In some cases, ES shells contain the capability to embed passwords. For example, Guru (Holsapple and Whinston [1987]) designed for use in a DOS environment, provides the designer with the ability to use passwords.

DOWNWARD DELEGATION—ACCESS TO DATA FILES

The problem of different levels of database security for the ES and the user is one of the primary problems of database access. One approach to this problem is to employ a database for each ES, ensuring that the ES database does not include any information that the set of users should not have access to. Controls can be established to ensure that the user cannot derive data for which the user does not have access (controls for the so-called derived data problem, e.g., Denning et al. [1987]). Controls can be built into the database to be aware of the "once-removed" nature of the ES user (there is an ES between the user and the database).

SOURCE OF THE DATA (PREVENT/DETECT USE OF WRONG KNOWLEDGE)

In some systems the ES solicits data from the user. If that data is incorrect then the wrong portion of the knowledge base will be searched. Thus, it is critical that the ES provide controls on the data it solicits. This can include traditional data edit controls, e.g., numeric field tests. In addition, it can include some specific application based reasonableness tests. Such tests could include analyses of relationships between submitted data items (e.g., of the type, pay rate times hours worked = total pay) or analytical tests of reasonableness.

PROGRAMMING SOFTWARE LIMITATIONS
(Prevent/detect use of knowledge to camouflage other activities)

Programming software might not meet the needs of the application, requiring special fixes and separate modules. If the software does not meet the needs then one control is to state that in the documentation of the system. In addition, another general control to this limitations is to require appropriate documentation of such special fixes and the expected behavior of those systems.

One approach to the prevention and detection of inappropriate use of special fixes is the use of so-called "intrusion-detection systems" (e.g., Denning [1987] and Tenor [1988]). These system are additional computer programs designed to monitor use of systems for unusual activity. Such unusual activity may include unusual computer program activity (as would occur with a Trojan horse program) or unusual user activity (use of a system at an unusual time in the day or for an unusual purpose). These systems are called intrusion-detection systems because they are designed to either detect intrusions or prevent them.

Summary

Although expert systems are computer programs, they are not the same as other computer programs because of the knowledge contained in them. Some unique characteristics of expert systems, deriving from the expert's knowledge embedded in them, was compared to other computer programs. General and application controls were developed for each of those unique characteristics.

In addition, issues underlying the audit of and security for Expert Systems were discussed. Both opportunities and challenges await internal auditors as they begin to develop standards and audit procedures to ES technologies.

References

Bull, M., et al. "Applying Software Engineering Principles to Knowlege Base Development." In *Proceedings of the First Annual Conference on Expert Systems in Business,* 27-38. New York: Learned Information, Nov. 1987.

Davis, D. "Artificial Intelligence Goes to Work." *High Technology,* April, 1987.

Denning D. "An Intrusion Detection Model." In *IEEE Transactions on Software Engineering,* vol. SE 14, no. 3, 252-261. New York: Institute of Electrical and Electronics Engineers, March 1987.

———, et al. "Views for Multilevel Databases." In *IEEE Transactions on Software Engineering,* vol. SE 13, no. 2, 129-139. New York:

Institute of Electrical and Electronics Engineers, February, 1987.

Fox, M. "Artificial Intelligence in Knowledge Representation." In *Proceedings of the Sixth International Joint Conference on Artificial Intelligence,* vol. 1, 282-284. Palo Alto, Calif.: Morgan Kaufmann, 1979.

Halper, S., G. Davis, P.J. O'Neil-Dunne, and P. Pfau. *Handbook of EDP Auditing.* Boston, Mass.: Warren, Gorham & Lamont, 1985.

Holsapple, C. and Whinston, A. *Business Expert Systems.* Homewood, Ill.: Irwin, 1987.

Jamieson, R. "Perspectives on Auditing Knowledge Based Systems." *Expert Systems in Business and Finance,* Chichester: John Wiley & Sons, Ltd., 1993, 249-266.

Kick, R. "Auditing an Expert System." *Expert Sytems,* Summer 1989, 33-38.

Lethan, H. and H. Jacobsen. "ESKORT—An Expert System for Auditing VAT Accounts." In *Proceedings of Expert Systems and Their Applications.* Avignon, France 1987.

McKee T. "An Audit Framework for Expert Systems." *Expert Systems Review* 2 (no. 4, 1991).

Michaelsen, R. *A Knowledge-based System for Individual Income and Transfer Tax Planning.* Champaign, Ill.: University of Illinois, 1991.

Moeller, R. "Expert Systems: Auditability Issues." *Expert Systems in Business and Finance.* Chichester: John Wiley & Sons, Ltd., 1993, 233-248.

Nazareth, D. "Issues in the Verification of Knowledge in Rule-based Systems." *International Journal of Man-Machine Studies* 30 (1989), 255-271.

Nyguyen T., W. Perkins, T. Lafferty, and D. Percora. "Knowledge-based Verification." *AI Magazine* 8 (no. 2, 1987).

O'Leary, D., 1987. "Validation of Expert Systems: With Applications to Accounting and Auditing." *Decision Sciences* 17 (no. 3), 468-486.

———, 1988a. "Expert Systems Prototyping as a Research Tool." In E. Turban and P. Watkins, *Applied Expert Systems,* Amsterdam: North-Holland, 1988.

———, 1988b. "Methods of Validating Expert Systems." *Interfaces* 18 (no. 6), 72-79.

141

————, 1988c. "Software Engineering and Research Issues in Accounting Information Systems," *Journal of Information Systems* 2 (no. 2, Spring 1988).

————, 1990a. "Soliciting Weights or Probabilities from Experts for Rule-Based Expert Systems." *International Journal of Man-Machine Studies* 32 (1990), 293-301.

————, 1990b. "Verification of Frames and Semantic Network Knowledge Bases." In *Proceedings of the 5th Knowledge Acquisition for Knowledge-based Systems Workshop,* Banff, Alta., Nov. 1990.

————, 1991a. "Design, Development and Validation of Expert Systems: A Survey of Developers." In *Verification, Validation and Testing of Expert Systems.* New York: John Wiley, 1991.

————, 1991b. "Knowledge Discovery as a Threat to Database Security." In *Knowledge Discovery in Databases.* Cambridge, Mass.: MIT Press, 1991.

————, 1992. "Measuring the Quality of an Expert System's Performance." *European Journal of Operational Research,* Feb., 1991.

———— and N. Kandelin, "Validating the Weights in Rule-based Expert Systems: A Statistical Approach." *International Journal of Expert Systems* 1 (no. 3, 1988).

———— and P. Watkins. "Review of Expert Systems in Auditing." *Expert Systems Review* 2 (nos 1 and 2, 1989).

Ribar, G. "Development of an Expert System." *Expert Systems Review* 1 (no. 3, 1988).

Shatz, H., R. Strahs, and L. Campbell. "Expertax: The Issue of Long-Term Maintenance." In *Proceedings of the 3rd international Conference on Expert Systems,* 291-300. Oxford, England: Learned Information, June 1987.

Socha, W. "Problems in Auditing Expert Systems." *The EDP Audit, Control and Security Newsletter,* March 1988.

Tenor, W. "Expert Systems for Computer Security." *Expert Systems Review in Business and Accounting* 1 (no. 2, 1988).

Watne, D. and P. Turney. *Auditing EDP Systems,* Englewood Cliffs, N.J.: Prentice-Hall, 1990, 555-590.

Weber, R. EDP *Auditing.* New York: McGraw-Hill, 1988.

Chapter 9

EXECUTIVE SUMMARY: RESEARCH FINDINGS, THEMES AND RECOMMENDATIONS FOR INTERNAL AUDITIORS

Expert Systems (ES) constitute one area of application of artificial intelligence (AI). Advanced information systems technologies such as Expert Systems are increasingly being planned, developed and implemented in a variety of business, government and other entities. As these technologies gain momentum in organizations, management must have some idea of how to control, manage and effectively utilize them in the organization.

Internal auditors are involved in at least five general roles related to information technology: (1) auditors, (2) consumers, (3) developers, (4) managers, and (5) consultants to management. Internal auditors should be involved in issues and activites related to Expert Systems development in organizations not only from their own perspective as internal auditors but also to provide assistance to management.

Research Objectives

One major goal of this research is to address issues that internal auditors should be aware of in their roles as auditors, consumers, consultants, managers and developers of ES/AI technologies. Accordingly, three major research objectives were identified in the form of the following questions:

1. To what extent are internal auditors and their management benefiting from expert systems technology?

2. What are the issues and opportunities underlying expert systems design, development and implementation as perceived by internal auditors?

3. What are the issues concerning the control, audit and security of expert systems?

This research is issue oriented and is not directly concerned with detailed technical issues or programming languages, nor does it provide a comprehensive treatise on AI. The contributions of the research include: (1) insights into expert systems development activities provided by mini case-studies of internal auditor efforts in this area, (2) identification of crucial issues that internal auditors and their management should be concerned with as this technology becomes more common in organizations.

This report should be of direct interest not only to internal auditors and internal audit management, but to managment in general regarding concerns addressed to the acquisition and management of applied artificial intelligence technology. Others outside of internal auditing and general management may find this study useful, such as those involved in training and education, consultants, and public accounting firms.

Another major goal of this research is to investigate the issue of technology diffusion of AI/ES among internal auditors. In particular, the book identifies two different approaches to the analysis of technology adoption.

1. What factors lead to the adoption of AI/ES by internal auditors

2. What is factors in the adoption of AI/ES impact the status of internal auditors.

The final goal of this research was to generate an understanding of some of the issues and problems associated with the audit and security of AI/ES. This led to the analysis of questions concerning which systems should be audited and an investigation of controls for AI/ES.

As a result of reading and reviewing the material in this report, the reader should gain an awareness of the scope and depth of applied artificial intelligence activities in large U.S. organizations and the audit issues that arise in dealing with these technologies. New insights may be obtained concerning potential applications for the technology and which provide perspectives on the issues, opportunities and audit concerns/appreaoches for the technology.

Research Approach

A survey of approximately 3600 heads of internal audit functions of large U.S. firms and members of the Institute of Internal Auditors was undertaken. Eleven interviews were conducted with top-level internal auditors at a variety of firms ranging from financial services institutions to manufacturing firms to retail and information services companies. As a result of information gathered through the above techniques, a number of crucial issues for internal auditors with respect to expert systems have been identified. These issues and a subsequent summary of key themes with accompanying recommendations for future audit concerns and attention are now presented.

Research Findings: Issues Concerning ES/AI and Internal Auditing

Issues were identified within the context of 11 categories which internal auditors provided in the form of "open-ended" responses to questions on the survey questionnaire. These categories of issues include:

- Benefits, Positive Prognosis
- Timing, Conservative Views on ES/AI
- Education, Training and Awareness
- Logic and Knowledge Base Problems
- Identification of an Appropriate Audit Trail
- Dealing with Appropriate Standards
- Applications Programs, Acquisition of Technology
- ES/AI Development
- Lack of Proper Management and Other Support
- Resources - Time/Cost-Benefit/Management
- No New Problems - Extensions of "Old" Methods

Several major themes are implicit in the issues identified above, among which are the need for more information on ES/AI, the need for better and more training on advanced technologies like ES/AI, better commitment of top management, the need for standards and proper documentation, the need to establish audit trails for the technology and so on. Each of the above categories of issues is now briefly reviewed.

BENEFITS, POSITIVE PROGNOSIS AND RELATED ISSUES

The general theme of this section is that AI/ES will greatly benefit internal auditors and that it is just a matter of time. Many feel that auditors need to "get up to speed" as quickly as possible and become leaders in the implementation of this technology in organizations.

Several respondents suggested that auditing is a fertile area for AI/ES, but new skills and new ways of thinking are required. Auditors must participate in the development of AI/ES systems and be capable of auditing them. This will provide new challenges, perhaps more significant than EDP, for external and internal auditors. However, AI/ES systems are capable of significant payback when properly understood and utilized. Auditors will need to develop better risk models to determine which expert systems to audit. Proliferation will most likely be at such a rate that audit departments will have difficulty in just keeping current with what systems are being developed.

Auditors should derive a great benefit as users of expert systems. They will have access to more information quicker and with less effort. The audit process may not speed up appreciably because the auditor will be doing more analytical work and less detailed information scheduling and gathering.

Respondents noted that AI/ES are technologies in their infancy. They are having bursts of genius and growing pains. Ten years from now both will be integral parts of all quality accounting and/or audit systems. AI/ES is the new technology. Companies will need to utilize AI/ES or lose their competitive advantage. Auditing has an opportunity to be on the leading edge rather than trailing as in the past. This can only happen if the Universities take an active, forward looking approach in their curriculums and IIA, EDPAA (EDP Auditors Association), etc. decide to help find solutions.

Some felt that we are not using AI/ES as effectively as we should. It has good potential for reducing manual work load and provides opportunity to examine a much larger sample than manual procedures. To fall behind users in terms of AI/ES knowledge will be fatal for the auditing profession.

TIMING ISSUES AND CONSERVATIVE VIEWS ON ES/AI

Knowing when to embrace the technology and the applicability of the technology to internal auditors appears to be the major theme of this category. Some believe that it will be a fairly long period of time before most internal auditors will be able to utilize or benefit from the technology.

This skepticism seems to be the result of viewing expert systems as an unproven technology or a technology that is too difficult and complex for internal auditors to cope with. Some respondents believe that only the very largest firms will have the resources and ability to utilize ES technologies. Many respondents believe that humans will be adversely affected with the implementation of ES technologies since they may tend to de-humanize decision making and may encourage human users of such systems to stop thinking and questioning assumptions. Other respondents expressed concerns ranging from the notion that AI/ES is just a "fad" to others believing that investment in such technologies would not be cost/beneficial.

EDUCATION, TRAINING AND AWARENESS ISSUES

The major concerns expressed in this category have to do with the time and effort required to "keep up" with the technology and the perceived training difficulties and challenges. Fears are expressed relating to the perceived complexity of the ES and the resultant training efforts expected. Internal auditors need to understand the expert systems technology in depth before control issues can be adequately addressed.

A concern was expressed by a number of respondents about the lack of and need for professional organizations to develop and provide training courses and materials for internal auditors in areas of expert systems, particularly from an audit issues point of view. Also of concern to those responding was the need for training strategies within firms which would be forward looking and anticipate where expert systems and other technologies were moving so that proper training could be offered to internal auditors that would give them the "best" available information in assessing and utilizing the expert systems technology.

Auditors as developers, advisers to management and auditors of expert systems will encounter problems if their level of training and expertise does not keep pace with the technology. Companies will have to make a commitment to adequately staff and train auditors to function in an AI/ES environment. This will be the key to properly address the AI/ES issue.

Training is important to address now and gain experience so auditors are prepared to audit later. Auditors would benefit from developing an expert system so as to be familiar with issues such as: approach, documentation, testing, cost, reliability and etc.

Most auditors today know little about AI/ES; this research will help with such needed general education. More information relating to the topic needs to be made available to the people in the internal auditing profession (i.e., through the IIA). IIA and EDPAA could do a better job of promoting technology and giving auditors examples of systems so auditors can find ways to use this technology.

Some ways must be found for internal auditors to get the necessary training to be able to audit in the AI/ES environment. Budget constraints make this an absorbing task. What is needed is a commitment to staff training. Changing mix of personnel backgrounds from accounting/auditing to engineering/EDP must be addressed.

Concerns were expressed with always being a follower and not a leader or innovator of the technology. There is an acute need to keep abreast of AI/ES technology and scheduled use by firms. Several firms indicated that technology is again ahead of the audit/control community. Auditors continue to stay in a "catch-up" mode. One of the main issues will be continuation of playing "catch-up" with technology. For example, one of the "big 6" external audit firms is implementing a new system geared to the "computer age"—it is great for the age we have recently been in but fails to fit the age we are entering—this will inevitably be the pattern in the future as in the past.

LOGIC AND KNOWLEDGE BASE PROBLEMS

The general themes underlying logic problems have to do with issues such as verifying the logic of the system. Since expert systems are often developed using "shells" the decision making logic may not be clearly available or identifiable by auditors. In addition, the issues of whose logic and knowledge is being verified and what basis exists for that logic and/or knowledge are of concern. Even if the logic/knowledge is reasonable, in general, how do auditors determine if it is appropriate for a given application? Other themes include the difficulty in establishing the proper basis for the logic and tracing the logic paths in the ES programs.

The logic in expert systems is often dependent on the manner in which knowledge is represented in the expert system. A common form of representation of knowledge is through the use of if-then rules. The use of rules presents challenges in the minds of respondents such as: how to provide exhaustive testing of the rules; how to evaluate the interrelationship among the rules; how to insure that proper authorization exists and is utilized in the changing of the rules; and how to ensure that the rules are "correct" and the decision points are functioning properly. Thus, determining the overall "correctness" of the system for a given problem domain is perceived to be a major challenge for auditors. Related to the issues of "correctness" of the system are the issues of "sufficiency" of the system. That is, how can auditors be assured that the system contains the necessary and sufficient considerations for providing advice in a particular application area?

Closely related to the notion of inference in the ES is the factual, procedural and domain knowledge represented in the system. Since internal auditors are more familiar in auditing procedures, policies and standards, auditing of a "knowledge" base will present new challenges. Among the challenges are the setting of standards for knowledge base evaluation. Issues of adequacy of knowledge and relationship of knowledge quality to decision outputs will be crucial for internal audit consideration.

ISSUES CONCERNED WITH IDENTIFICATION OF PROPER AUDIT TRAIL

A general theme in this category is the general difficulty in identifying and establishing a proper audit trail for ES.

For example, some respondents expressed concern about the potential lack of documentation standards over updates to the knowledge base which would present concerns with respect to an adequate audit trail. Additional audit trail concerns were expressed due to the complexity of some expert systems which don't facilitate easy identification of audit trails. The potential difficulty in verifying the audit trail components of the expert system were also cited due to inexperience of both developers and auditor of expert systems.

AI/ES technologies are similar to computers in general and more recently PCs. The people using them will resist putting in effective controls at the start and therefore the ability to use, update, review and manage and audit such applications will become very difficult during their early lives.

ISSUES DEALING WITH APPROPRIATE STANDARDS

With a new technology, standards do not exist and the appropriate development of such standards is perceived to be a problem. Since there are no generally agreed upon standards for documentation and terminology for AI/ES, difficulties will exist in setting evaluation standards. In addition, the newness of the technology makes it difficult to evaluate initial projects in AI/ES due to the lack of established, agreed upon standards.

When rule based routines are integrated into large scale transaction systems (AMEX's credit analyzer), how they drive other traditional elements of the computer support function and how they are installed, certified for wide domain use, and monitored will be critical issues which will merge with the broader issues of application migration on to networks and cooperative processing controls between computers of different scale and architecture.

APPLICATIONS PROGRAMS AND ACQUISITION OF TECHNOLOGY ISSUES

Major concerns appear to be cost and availability issues. Due to anticipated high costs and lack of readily useful commercial products some respondents appear to be dubious about the utility of ES in their areas. They cite the costs and time for development of in-house tools and want to "wait and see" what commercial vendors can develop for "off-the-shelf" purchase by internal audit groups. Also noted was a general notion of the desirability of off-the-shelf products to facilitate easier utilization of the technology and eliminate some of the perceived high costs of development and training. This acquisition of commercial products also presents potential problems such as vendors' capabilities and willingness to produce reliable logic engines that are controllable and maintain their integrity. Other concerns included the specific nature of AI/ES and the difficulty in finding general purpose application areas for which AI/ES makes sense.

More information is needed from those who have had successful/unsuccessful experiences with AI/ES applications. Also, more information is need about packages available. Since development is costly, some auditors will be looking for "developed" systems from the IIA - professional accounting bodies, etc.

Typical audit departments will not invest any time and effort in developing ES. They will more likely purchase ES packages from vendors.

DEVELOPMENT ISSUES

The nature of ES is different from conventional systems and a perceived need is how to extend current capabilities and technology to incorporate the "new" technology. Respondents were especially concerned with the proliferation of end-user computing on micros and workstations and the availability of ES shells which facilitate experimentation and ultimately business use without input or involvement from internal auditors. The potential for rapid growth of ES at the end-user level due to proliferation of micros also presents potential audit backlog if internal auditing becomes involved in attempting to establish controls and audit procedures for these systems.

Typically, ES development utilizes prototyping which results in faster development but makes it difficult for internal auditors to be involved in the entire development process. If internal auditors were to assert the need for involvement at the prototyping phase of development, respondents believed that strong resistance would be encountered from the development team since such involvement would slow the development process considerably. In addition, since much ES development does not follow the traditional systems development life cycle (SDLC), reviewing procedures tend to be highly subjective and judgmental.

The use of Expert Systems introduces questions of ownership for system functions as well as ongoing data integrity. Is the system to be maintained by the Expert who designed it, or the developer who built it, or both? As the system matures and "rules" become more complex or just increase, maintenance becomes a significant cost factor. This should be considered during design and system development.

The difficulty to define appropriate areas for which to apply the AI/ES technologies is also of concern. Extracting relevant data from human experiences (expertise) for maintaining as well as developing the system presents many new challenges.

LACK OF PROPER MANAGEMENT AND OTHER SUPPORT

The general theme of this category appears to be fear of being able to "sell" the idea of ES to management and getting management commitment and support. Some respondents suggest that selling any system to management is a problem and AI/ES will be "just that more difficult".

Other respondents noted that internal audit functions are typically understaffed and with new technologies such as AI/ES, finding staff to deal with the new challenges brought about by these technologies will be extremely difficult. Some respondents felt that this technology was beyond the scope of the audit function due to lack of management support and should be addressed by the MIS professionals in the organization. These respondents cited as examples the case where EDP audit has not been given much respect by management in traditional systems areas due to a lack of understanding by management and thus the MIS group has control

Getting the support of management, in general, for audits has been difficult and to get management support for a new technology will be even more difficult is the view of some respondents. Most respondents agree that getting senior management's support and commitment is critical to internal audit success in dealing with AI/ES issues.

RESOURCES—TIME/COST-BENEFIT/MANAGEMENT

The major problems of lack of staff, lack of budget and lack of time are identified as the major constraints to ES development. In the area of costs several respondents pointed out that given the speed at which AI/ES technology is changing that committing large financial resources for the acquisition of AI hardware/software is not cost effective. Many respondents cited the lack of satisfactory cost/benefit ratios and the difficulty in measuring the benefits realized from AI/ES.

Another major concern was the lack of internal audit staff especially in light of the perceived time requirements for AI/ES related activities. Since the perceived time requirements are great, experienced auditors may be unwilling to invest the time necessary to become proficient in the AI/ES areas.

In large firms where use of ES shells are becoming widespread, some respondents expressed the concern that duplication of effort and resources in multiple areas of the firm which are developing AI/ES would ultimately have a negative impact on the organization by inadequate utilization of resources. This, and the fact that most ES are unique and cannot be utilized outside of the domain for which they were developed makes resource issues of primary concern.

Another key concern is the large development time for ES/AI technology and the general lack of time by internal auditors to accomplish current task loads. Several respondents suggested that budget was not the problem but lack of personnel who might be involved with AI/ES is a major problem. Since little is known about development activities for ES in other organizations, there is some concern that maintenance and documentation may be very time consuming and costly. Respondents from smaller firms expressed concerns with whether of not they would ever be able to embrace the technology due to resource constraints.

Separation of manpower between audit and management information systems is also of concern. The current situation in many firms is not good for relying on existing MIS manpower for internal audit projects. Sufficient initiated projects must be from within internal audit.

NO NEW PROBLEMS—JUST EXTENSION OF CURRENT TECHNOLOGY/METHODS

This category deals with perceived issues relating to the "new" technology of Expert Systems. Most auditors expressed the view that Expert Systems are just extensions of current technology and that basically no new problems are anticipated. Several respondents felt that the problems with expert systems were not really new but analogous to the migration from batch to real-time systems, that is, going from a paper audit trail to a hidden or nonexistent audit trail. Other respondents used the analogy of moving from auditing around the computer to auditing through the computer as a basis of comparison for "new" problems anticipated in moving to expert systems: that is, no really new problems just a requirement for a change in thinking an understanding the environment plus new techniques.

Although not presenting new problems for auditors per se, some respondents felt that management would have difficulty initially understanding issues such as increased scope of audits encompassing expert systems and the need for review of rules in systems, and assessing the validity of choices of experts who provide expertise for expert systems.

Key Themes and Recommendations for Further Internal Auditor Consideration

The issues derived from the interviews and the surveys are developed into a summary of key themes that internal auditors should consider. These themes encompass those issues discussed in the previous section and range from audit issues to broader issues such as knowledge maintenance and management control. Additional support for the themes was derived in part from a review of the Expert Systems and auditing literature (See Appendix A), prior studies of Expert Systems and auditing, and the interview results of this study.

The resulting themes and associated recommendations may be used to guide internal auditors as they investigate, plan, develop, use and audit ES/AI technologies. These themes focus attention on specific areas of concern and opportunities for internal auditors. Recommendations also provide guidance to internal auditors to enable perspective and approaches/solutions to these key themes to be addressed.

THEME 1: TECHNOLOGY TRANSFER

- How to Transfer ES/AI Technologies to Internal Audit Functions
- How to Obtain and Manage Scarce Resources
- How to Train and Educate Audit Staffs in New Technologies
- How to Monitor and Keep Abreast of New Developments

A major concern of internal auditors is "keeping up" with technology. With limited budgets, time and staff, the challenge of embracing a new technology appears most challenging. Many firms who have adequate budgets may not have adequate time and firms who have large staffs, may not have the necessary resources to divert those staff from audit projects to technology projects. Utilizing the MIS or AI professionals within other areas of the firm may not be effective due to backlogs and shortages of resources within those areas.

Related to resource issues is the issue of acquiring the requisite knowledge to properly effect the technology transfer. Both interviewees and survey respondents indicated the need for more information ranging from how to get started to demanding to see sample applications to asking for a stronger role of professional associations such as the IIA in disseminating such information. A major conclusion of this research is the need to provide more focused, selective information on using AI/ES technologies in the many diverse roles of internal auditors.

As ES/AI technologies become more widespread and desirable, the role of the internal auditor will broaden and require a whole new set of technical and auditing skills which augment the current training and expertise.

RECOMMENDATIONS—TECHNOLOGY TRANSFER

1. Start out with small, manageable projects.

2. Experiment and develop prototypes using "off-the-shelf" shells—this will demonstrate feasibility and help gain support of higher level management.

3. Take advantage of continuing education programs offered through professional associations and societies and university seminars—if these groups don't offer what you desire, let them know.

4. Utilize joint projects with other in-house groups or with outside consultants—minimizes risk, less long term tie-up and consumption of resources, may have more immediate payoff.

THEME 2: AUDITABILITY AND CONTROL ISSUES OF ES/AI TECHNOLOGIES

Many internal auditors expressed concern with the challenges brought about by ES/AI systems which have complex logic and knowledge base components. Many expressed the need to develop new audit methodologies and techniques for pursuing these technologies. At this point, most firms do not have procedures, plans or methods for auditing complex ES/AI techniques. This will need to become a high priority issue for firms embracing the ES/AI technology. Other concerns deal with controls over the design and development activities of ES/AI systems and proper documentation and control standards.

RECOMMENDATIONS—AUDITABILITY/CONTROL

1. Clearly determine and define what constitutes Expert Systems in a "pure or true" sense (as defined in Section 1 of this report). This will to a large extent enable clearer definition of the appropriate auditing methods to be employed. Many respondents to the survey seemed to have widely ranging concepts of what constituted an ES. Many believed that ES had to have human expertise within and to operate at the level of human experts. Others simply viewed them as enhanced embedded audit routines and/or decision aids with little or no human expertise or sophisticated knowledge. ES/AI systems at the low end will not require much in the way of new audit methodologies. On the other hand, at the high end, ES which replicate human judgment may well need to have advanced and more thorough audit methodologies.

2. Insist on being part of the design, development team that builds ES which require audit elements. Some efforts will be required to assess quality, validity of knowledge bases and inference mechanisms.

155

3. Begin now to develop general frameworks of control standards for ES/AI environments. This will include documentation standards, review standards and definitional standards. Recognize that these standards may well be dynamic and require routine monitoring and adjustment, given the tenancy for most ES to be of a dynamic nature.

THEME 3: MONITORING, MAINTENANCE AND ENHANCEMENT ISSUES

ES/AI systems tend to be dynamic and require almost constant attention to maintain the knowledge components. Additionally, constant monitoring of the quality and efficacy of the advice rendered by the system must also be addressed. Unlike conventional systems, ES are rarely, if ever, completed. That is, due to the constant effort to fine tune performance and augment, enhance the knowledge base, these systems continue to evolve over time. The maintenance issue of the knowledge base is critical since the maintenance activity not only affects the content of the knowledge base but has the potential to interact with other aspects of the system and other systems and cause assumptions and results to change over time.

RECOMMENDATIONS: MONITORING/MAINTENANCE

1. Attention must be given to the creation of a knowledge base guru, much in principle like a database administrator. One difficulty with this task is that ES tend to be highly specialized where databases are usually quite general. This may suggest that multiple knowledge base administrators need to be appointed, each one for a particular ES. A second difficulty with the knowledge base administration function is the skills requirement of the individual. For example, in an internal audit function, the knowledge base administrator may be required to have extensive knowledge of a particular aspect of internal auditing, a sophisticated knowledge of expert systems in general and the particular ES under consideration, a general knowledge of the environment in which the ES operates and the potential impact of changes to the ES knowledge base on other systems and assumptions within the environment. Such individuals are in short supply.

2. Attention must be given to change attitudes toward ES technology in the sense that the systems are dynamic and some-

what fragile. Some of the interviewees suggested that a tendency, once an ES is designed and developed is to place undo reliance on that system and accept its advice without question or challenge. Proper educational programs and training must be established as well as policies to ensure that the ES advice is given proper scrutiny; and unquestioned reliance on the ES is avoided.

3. Attention must be given and management must recognize that ES must be maintained. Depending on the domain, some effort must be made to constantly be aware of new knowledge, and assumptions that will change, augment or cause the knowledge base to need to be refined.

THEME 4: "OFF-THE-SHELF" APPLICATIONS SOFTWARE VERSUS CUSTOM DESIGNED, DEVELOPED SOFTWARE ISSUES

Many of the participants in this study expressed the desire/need for ready made ES applications software citing a lack of time and other resources which would preclude in-house development of such systems. Care must be taken in considering this issue since ES typically are not generalizable. That is, an ES is usually designed for a specific task within a specific environment. This is not to say that there are some areas, perhaps in internal auditing, where generalizable packages may be feasible but to caution against unrealistic expectations. While off-the-shelf software may have some appeal from a resource point of view, it, in the long run, may provide more difficulties and challenges since it was designed for the particular task at hand.

RECOMMENDATIONS—"OFF-THE-SHELF" SOFTWARE

1. Expert Systems Shells offer a compromise position between ready-made applications and custom developed, from-scratch systems. ES shells allow fast prototyping and facilitate experimentation at relatively low cost and risk. Once shells have been developed, then appropriate decisions can be made regarding the develop-from-scratch approach or continued utilization of the shell. The shell is off-the-shelf component and the knowledge base is the custom component. What is lacking is often the ability to customize the user interface, inference component, interface to other systems and so on.

2. Be wary of off-the-shelf systems which promise to be general problem solvers. Require any such programs to furnish complete documentation regarding the inference structure and content of the knowledge base. The challenge is greater for auditors of off-the-shelf ES since often the knowledge component is proprietary and an auditor's ability to assess the reasonableness of the knowledge and inference component is highly restricted.

THEME 5: TRENDS, INTEGRATION AND EXPECTATIONS VERSUS REALITY ISSUES

There has been much hype and promises with respect to ES/AI. Be wary of these systems but at the same time recognize that they are being used successfully in internal audit and other business activities. Many participants in this study expressed reservations about the efficacy of ES for internal auditing while others were generally enthusiastic. Some middle ground is probably where the true state of ES technologies is at present. Those with negative feelings toward ES technology probably need to become acquainted with a few success stories and those with wild expectations need to become acquainted with a few failure stories of ES implementation. At this point in time ES/AI technologies may be viewed as a logical and natural extension of existing information systems/technologies. ES simply extend current software/programs and thus auditors should consider them extensions and evolutionary, not revolutionary in nature. Clearly, the issue of integration of ES/AI technologies into existing systems is a major issue and will continue to be so for the next few years. At that point we will tend not to think of ES/AI systems as distinct but rather as just a dimension or component of a current system.

OTHER THEMES:

Many other themes could be developed. The issues identified previously provide some basis for looking at a wide range of issues. The above five themes are therefore not deemed to be all inclusive but simply designed to capture some of the dominant themes identified in the research. What is evident from this study are the following general points in addition to the major themes above:

1. ES are becoming more widely used in internal auditing.

2. There is a great desire for more information and training on ES technologies (within Internal Audit).

3. A great many applications are foreseen for the ES/AI technologies in internal auditing.

4. A number of constraints exist which limit the more rapid development, employment of these systems: personnel, time, top management support and budget.

5. Perceived benefits are many and the majority of the participants in the study are quite positive about the prognosis for ES applications in internal auditing.

6. Virtually no work has been undertaken to develop standards audit procedures and so on for ES/AI technologies whether within internal audit or other functional areas of the firms.

7. There is a great deal of interest in ES/AI by internal audit heads (as evidenced by the quantity and quality of the response to this research project). But at the same time there is some uneasiness in knowing what the right place to be at this time is, given the current environments of the firm, market and capabilities of the technology.

8. ES activity is not limited to the largest multinational firms. Firms of all sizes from one person audit departments to 500 person audit departments are concerned/interested in ES issues.

Appendix A—Survey Questionnaire

INSTITUTE OF INTERNAL AUDITORS RESEARCH PROJECT ON THE APPLICATION OF ARTIFICIAL INTELLIGENCE AND EXPERT SYSTEMS IN INTERNAL AUDITING

This questionnaire is designed to gather your opinions concerning the use of artificial intelligence (AI) and expert systems (ES) in your firm, particularly as it affects the internal audit function. Internal auditors typically not only serve in an audit function, but as consultants to management, as users of advanced technologies and as designers and developers of technologies such as AI/ES.

Please respond as appropriate and return the questionnaire in the self-addressed envelope as soon as possible but prior to July 10, 1988.

Please return the questionnaire to:
Professor Daniel O'Leary
USC
School of Accounting,
Los Angeles, CA 90089-1421

1. Please indicate the approximate annual sales for your firm.

   _____

2. Please indicate the general type of industry in which you would classify your firm, for example, financial services, high technology, aerospace, etc.

   _____

3. Please indicate the approximate number of employees in the

   Internal audit function (excluding EDP)

   _____

EDP audit function

---

4. Please indicate the degree of general familiarity you have with artificial intelligence and/or expert systems. (Check the appropriate response below)

   ❏ No Familiarity ❏ Low Familiarity ❏ Moderate Familiarity
   ❏ High Familiarity

5. To what extent are you employing expert systems, artificial intelligence technologies as part of the internal audit function? (Check the appropriate response below)

   ❏ None ❏ Low ❏ Moderate ❏ High

6. To what extent is the internal audit function involved in providing input for management decisions regarding acquisition, development, and usage of artificial intelligence/expert systems in your firm? (Check the appropriate response below)

   ❏ None ❏ Low ❏ Moderate ❏ High

7. To what extent is the internal audit function developing policies, procedures and plans for dealing with issues related to artificial intelligence/expert systems technologies in the firm? (Check the appropriate response below)

   ❏ None ❏ Low ❏ Moderate ❏ High

8. Please indicate the areas below which you believe have potential for the application of artificial intelligence/expert systems technologies in support of internal auditing in your firm. (Check all that apply.)

   ❏ Embedded Audit Routines   ❏ Smart Questionnaires
   ❏ Financial Fraud Detection   ❏ Audit Planning
   ❏ Audit Risk Assessment   ❏ Analytical Review Assessment
   ❏ Personnel Scheduling   ❏ Decison Aids

9. How many AI/ES applications are you:

   Using____ Developing____ Planning____ Not Utilizing____

10. Please indicate the AI/ES development environment you are utilizing: (Check the appropriate response below)

    Hardware: ❏ Micro/Mini ❏ Micro/Mini/Mainframe
    ❏ Mainframe

    Software: ❏ ES Shells ❏ LISP/Prolog ❏ Other

11. If the internal audit function has been involved or is going to be involved in designing, developing and implementing expert systems technologies, how did (do) you plan to acquire the expertise necessary to proceed? (Check all that apply.)

    ❏ Train Current Staff ❏ Utilize Outside Consultants
    ❏ Hire AI/ES Experts
    ❏ Jointly Funded Project with Outside Consultants

12. If your firm has or is planning to develop an expert system, please indicate the types of expert systems applications that you had previously heard of. (Check all that apply.)

    ❏ Medical ❏ Accounting ❏ Auditing ❏ Tax
    ❏ Internal Auditing ❏ Other

13. Is there a firmwide "pressure" to adopt the use of expert systems technologies into departments within your firm, including Internal Auditing? (Please check your response.)

    ❏ None ❏ Some ❏ Extensive

14. How true are the following statements? Please check your response for each statement.

    a. Budgetary pressures make it impossible to spend any resources on expert systems in internal auditing.

    ❏ Not True ❏ Somewhat ❏ True

b. There is substantial support available internally for the development of expert systems.

❏ Not True   ❏ Somewhat   ❏ True

c. Expert systems offer substantial advantages in terms of reducing manpower needs over current manual methods.

❏ Not True   ❏ Somewhat   ❏ True

d. There is substantial uncertainty that expert systems can improve the audit process.

❏ Not True   ❏ Somewhat   ❏ True

e. Expert systems developed to date have had very good success.

❏ Not True   ❏ Somewhat   ❏ True

f. Internal audit expert systems have substantial opportunity to disrupt the operations of the firm beyond the scope of the internal audit department.

❏ Not True   ❏ Somewhat   ❏ True

g. There has been substantial information flow from organizations such as the IIA and the EDPAA regarding the use of expert systems in accounting.

❏ Not True   ❏ Somewhat   ❏ True

h. Suitable expert systems can be built for use in internal auditing using inexpensive (e.g., $300) expert systems shells.

❏ Not True   ❏ Somewhat   ❏ True

i. Expert systems in internal audit improve the status of internal auditors.

❏ Not True   ❏ Somewhat   ❏ True

15. What benefits/obstacles do you currently experience or anticipate experiencing from use of AI/ES technologies in the internal audit function of your firm? (Check all that apply)

BENEFITS

❏ Cost Savings

❏ More Timely Decision
Making

❏ More Confident Decision
Making

❏ Reduced Labor Cost

❏ More Rapid Development
NoviceEmployees

❏ Enhanced Ability to
Constantly Monitor
Complex Situations

❏ More Efficient Utilization
of Existing Audit Expertise

❏ Enhanced Image as
Technology Leader

❏ Migrating Applications
from Internal Audit to Operations

OBSTACLES

❏ Identifying/Extracting
Expertise for Developing
Expert Systems

❏ Open Ended Nature of Some
AI/ES Projects

❏ Long Development Cycles

❏ Difficult to Define Appropriate
Areas for Which to ApplyAI/ES

❏ Inadequate Computer of
Resources

❏ Lack of Budget Resources

❏ Lack of Trained Personnel

❏ Selling Management on AI/ES
for Internal Audit

16. To what extent do you anticipate new problems in auditing and
securing expert systems. Please explain your response.

17. Please make any open-ended comments you wish concerning artificial intelligence/expert systems technologies and the issues which
internal auditors will face in dealing with these tech-nologies as
users, developers, advisers to management and as auditors:

18. If we may call you to obtain more information, please complete the
information below:
Name/Title _____
Company _____
Address _____
City/State/Zip_____
Telephone Number _____

Table A-1

MEANS, STANDARD DEVIATIONS AND RANGES FOR RESPONSES TO EACH QUESTION ON THE SURVEY INSTRUMENT

Variable Name	Mean	Std. Dev.	Min. Value	Max. Value
Total Auditors	26.34	53.92	0	50
EDP Auditors	4.71	78.856	0	80
Industry	6.35	6.31	1	20
Familiarity	1.52	0.56	1	3
Employing ES	0.4	0.66	0	3
Input to Management	0.61	0.75	0	3
Policies for ES	0.55	0.73	0	3
Embedded Routines	62.00	0.49	0	1
Smart Questionnaire	0.78	0.41	0	1
Fraud Detection	0.40	0.49	0	1
Audit Planning	0.53	0.50	0	1
Audit Risk	0.75	0.43	0	1
Analytical Review Procedures	0.46	0.50	0	1
Personnel Scheduling	0.28	0.45	0	1
Decision Making	0.38	0.64	0	1
Using ES	0.56	2.32	0	40
Developing ES	0.24	0.82	0	8
Planning ES	0.45	1.12	0	10
Not using ES	0.31	0.51	0	4
Micro	0.24	0.51	0	6
Both Micro/Mainframe	0.20	0.40	0	1
Mainframe	0.05	0.22	0	1
Shells	0.25	0.44	0	1
LISP	0.06	0.24	0	1
Train Staff	0.51	0.50	0	1
Consultants	0.21	0.41	0	1
Hire AI Experts	0.05	0.22	0	1

(Table A-1 continued)

Joint Projects	0.05	0.22	0	1
Medical ES	0.26	0.44	0	1
Accounting ES	0.25	0.44	0	1
Auditing ES	0.33	0.47	0	1
Taxes	0.26	0.44	0	1
Internal Audit	0.34	0.48	0	1
Pressure	−0.70	0.49	−1	1
Budget	−0.22	0.69	−1	1
Support	−0.54	0.61	−1	1
Manpower	−0.02	0.61	−1	1
Uncertainty-	−0.14	0.70	−1	1
Success	−0.12	0.54	−1	1
Disrupt	−0.58	0.60	−1	1
Flow of Information	−0.48	0.63	−1	1
Suitable	−0.06	0.63	−1	1
Status	0.01	0.69	−1	1
Cost Saving	0.39	0.49	0	1
Timely Decision Making	0.47	0.50	0	1
Confident Decision Making	0.57	0.50	0	1
Labor Saving	0.27	0.45	0	1
Rapid Development	0.44	0.50	0	1
Enhanced Monitoring	0.51	0.50	0	1
Efficient Utilization	0.63	0.48	0	1
Image	0.33	0.47	0	1
Migration	0.18	0.39	0	1
Selling Management	0.39	0.49	0	1
Lack of Personnel	0.66	0.47	0	1
No Budget	0.49	0.50	0	1
Inadequate Compensation	0.20	0.40	0	1
Define Areas	0.44	0.50	0	1
Long Development	0.41	0.49	0	1
Open-ended Nature	0.29	0.46	0	1
Extract Expertise	0.57	0.72	0	1

Appendix B
Statistical Analysis of Survey Results

SPECIFIC EFFECTS OF SURVEY RESULTS

The prior material in chapter 4 of the book on the survey results focused on the general responses to the survey questions. It was also desired in this research to see what effect, if any, size, degree of familiarity and industry membership had on the survey results.

SIZE

To evaluate the effects of size on various responses the total number of auditors and the total number of EDP auditors obtained in response to question 3 were used as surrogates for size. Regression analysis, a statistical technique for evaluating the relationship between two or more variables was utilized to see what relationship might exist between the size variables and the remaining variables indicated by the remaining questions on the survey instrument. Two regressions were run: (1) a regression of total auditors on the remaining questionnaire responses and (2) a regression of EDP auditors on the remaining questionnaire responses. Table B-1 shows the results for the regression of total auditors on the remaining questions of the survey and Table B-2 shows the results of the regression of number of EDP auditors on the remaining questions of the survey instrument. The degree of familiarity with ES/AI concepts and the remaining questionnaire items was analyzed with regression analysis. These results are presented in Table B-3.

The degree of familiarity with AI/ES and the relationship between the remaining questions was also submitted to a specialized analysis for dealing with categorical response data. This analysis is known as a log-linear analysis and is similar to analysis of variance (ANOVA) when the responses are all categorical. One goal of this analysis was to see if industry classification and/or degree had any effect on the response to any individual question's response.

Industry was only significant in explaining question 14d: There is substantial uncertainty that expert systems can improve the audit process. Thus, the "true, not true" responses to this question are related to industry. Interestingly, the most important factors in explaining responses to question 14d were industry classification and degree of familiarity.

Table B-1

RELATIONSHIP BETWEEN THE TOTAL NUMBER
OF AUDITORS ON AND THE REMAINING
QUESTIONNAIRE RESPONSES

Mean Value of Total Number of Auditors: 26.34

Questions that are related to the total number of auditors:
Degree of Relation (+ or −)

Q7: Involvement of Internal Auditors in Developing Policies
Related to AI +

Q8a: Embedded audit routines as a potential application for
ES/AI +

Q8g: Personnel scheduling as a potential application for
ES/AI −

Q9b: Number of ES/AI being developed +

Q9c: Number of ES/AI being planned +

Q10a: Hardware development environment is mostly
micro/mini computers −

Q12c: Have previously heard of auditing ES/AI applications +

Q13: Firm−Wide pressure to adopt the use of ES/AI
technologies +

Q14b: Substantial support internally for developing AI/ES +

Q14d: Substantial uncertainty expert systems can improve
audit process +

Q14h: Suitable ES can be built using inexpensive shells −

Q15b: Benefit is more timely decision making +

Q15g: Obstacle of open−ended nature of some AI/ES +

Note: The degree of Relation Column shows the positive or negative
relationship between number of auditors and the given question

---

Table B-2

RELATIONSHIP BETWEEN THE NUMBER OF
EDP AUDITORS AND THE REMAINING
QUESTIONNAIRE RESPONSES

Mean Value of Number of EDP Auditors: 4.72

Questions that are related to the total number of auditors: Degree
of Relation (+ or −)

Q3a: Total Number of Auditors (excluding EDP) +

Q8a: Embedded audit routines as a potential application for
ES/AI +

Q10a: Hardware development environment is mostly
micro/mini computers +

Q10c: Hardware development environment is most
mainframe −

Q10e: Software development environment is mostly shells +

Q11c: We plan to hire AI/ES experts to develop AI/ES
applications +

Q11d: We plan to enter into jointly funded projects with
consultants +

Q14g: Substantial information flow from IIA and others −

Q15b: Benefit is more timely decision making −

Degree of familiarity with AI/ES was important in many of the other questions and these results are shown in Table B-4. It was also desirous to see what the relationship was between industry categorization and the remaining questions. The regression analysis showed no significant relationships between industry and any of the remaining questions. This is supports the conclusions reached based on the log linear model building analysis of Table B-4.

Table B-5 presents the means of the responses to the questions of the questionnaire. This gives some insights, on an overall average basis, of how the respondents viewed the questions.

In general, the regressions show that the degree of familiarity

---

Table B-3

RELATIONSHIP BETWEEN DEGREE OF FAMILIARITY
WITH AI/ES AND THE REMAINING
QUESTIONNAIRE RESPONSES

Mean Value of Degree of Familiarity: 1.52

Questions that are related to the total number of auditors: Degree of Relation (+ or −)

Q5:   To what extent are you employing ES/AI in internal audit +

Q7:   Involvement of Internal Auditors in Developing Policies Related to AI +

Q9a: Number of ES/AI applications being used +

Q10a: Hardware development environment is mostly micro/mini computers +

Q10b: Hardware development environment is both micro/mainframe +

Q12c: Have previously heard of auditing ES/AI applications +

Q12d: Have previously heard of tax ES/AI applications +

Q15c: Benefit is more confident decision making +

Q15c: Obstacle is lack of budget resources +

---

with expert systems concepts "explains" some of the responses to the questions of the survey. Industry, size and other factors did not appear to be as important as the familiarity variable. Thus, one can conclude that the responses are generally not influenced by the size of the firm or the industry group represented by the firm. There is some relationship between how familiar the respondents are with ES and the actual answer given.

Note: The proposed model notation, for example, IFB, indicates a model where the responses are grouped in a table of industry by familiarity by particular question, both mainframe/micro. (The letter I indicates industry, F indicates degree of familiarity and the third letter is

Table B-4

BEST SETS OF MODELS IN EXPLAINING RESPONSES TO INDUSTRY CLASSIFICATION, DEGREE OF FAMILIARITY AND SPECIFIC QUESTION FROM SURVEY RESULTS

Question		Proposed Model	Best Model
Q10b:	Both Mainframe/Micro	IFB	F,B
Q14a:	Budgetary Pressures	IFB	F,B
Q9b:	Developing ES (number)	IFD	F*
Q14f:	Opportunity to Disrupt	IFD	F,D
Q14g:	Information Flow from IIA	IFF	F*
Q6:	Extent of Providing Inpu	IFI	F,I
Q10e:	Developing using LISP	IFL	F,L
Q10c:	Developing using Mainframe	IFM	F,M
Q14c:	ES Reduces Manpower Needs	IFM	F,M
Q10a:	Developing using Micros	IFM	F,M
Q8d:	Audit Planning Applications	IFP	F,P
Q7:	Developing Plans for AI/ES	IFP	F,P
Q13:	Pressure to Adopt ES/AI	IFP	F,P
Q10d:	Developing Using Shells	IFS	F,S
Q14e:	ES have had Good Success	IFS	F,S
Q14h:	Suitable ES using Shells	IFS	F,S
Q14b:	Support for ES	IFS	F,S
Q14d:	Uncertainty for ES	IFU	I,F**
Q9a:	Number of ES Using	IFU	F,U

* = *Degree of familiarity was the only important element in the proposed model.*
** = *Both industry and degree of familiarity were the most important elements in this proposed model.*

the first letter of a word representing a question. For example, the first proposed model in the table is IFB. B represents the "Both" keyword from question 10b.) Thus a full complement of all combinations of industry, familiarity and the particular question are evaluated. The "best" model notation indicates which subset of the full-model best explains the responses to the questions, given that we are considering industry and degree of familiarity, in addition to a particular question. For example, for question 9b above, the best model was F, degree of familiarity. Thus industry and the number of systems being developed were not as important as degree of familiarity in responding to the "How Many are You developing" question.

WARNER MEMORIAL LIBRARY
EASTERN COLLEGE
ST. DAVIDS, PA. 19087